Lionel FasTrack
Model Railroads

Lionel FasTrack Model Railroads

The Easy Way to Build a Realistic Lionel Layout

Robert Schleicher

Voyageur Press

First published in 2009 by Voyageur Press, an imprint of MBI Publishing Company,
400 First Avenue North, Suite 300, Minneapolis, MN 55401 USA

Voyageur Press titles are also available at discounts in bulk quantity
for industrial or sales-promotional use. For details write to Special Sales Manager
at MBI Publishing Company, 400 First Avenue North, Suite 300, Minneapolis, MN 55401 USA.

To find out more about our books, visit us online at www.voyageurpress.com.

Library of Congress Cataloging-in-Publication Data

Schleicher, Robert H.
Lionel FasTrack model railroads: The easy way to build a
realistic Lionel layout / Robert Schleicher.–1st ed.
p. cm.
Includes index.
ISBN 978-0-7603-3590-1 (sb : alk. paper)
1. Railroads–Models. 2. Lionel L.L.C. I. Title.
TF197.S3387 2009
625.1'9–dc22
2008036096

Designer: John P. Sticha

Printed in Singapore

Contents

CHAPTER 1

Lionel FasTrack Layouts

You expect Lionel to provide a simple model railroad system, one that even an older child can assemble successfully. And so it does, thanks in part to the clever design of the brand's track and electric control systems, which are designed to be operated on the living room floor or on a dedicated tabletop. You can assemble the layout of your dreams, take it apart to reassemble the next one, and be assured that each layout will operate as realistically and reliably as the first.

Facing page: Steve Sherman and his crew from Quality Machine Solutions in Enfield, Connecticut, created the sheer rock cliff scenery for Mark Cavaliere's FasTrack layout (Chapter 14).

Any Lionel O-27 or O scale locomotive or car from the past 100 years will operate on FasTrack, including the incredibly detailed O scale EMD F3A like this one from Bill Langsdorf's layout (Chapter 13).

Lionel has been stamping three-rail track from sheet-steel strips for more than a century, and their all-steel track can still be purchased today, but Lionel FasTrack really is the Lionel track for the new millennium. Lionel had offered alternate track systems before, but none of them were any better, in balance, than the all-steel stuff. FasTrack, however, is almost as rugged as the all-steel track, easier to assemble and disassemble, and looks like real railroad track. Furthermore, FasTrack is not just track and switches—it's an entire track system.

FasTrack Assembly

FasTrack is quick to assemble and even quicker to disassemble. The original Lionel all-steel track is rugged, and it takes a bit of strength to force the tight-fitting pins into the hollow rails. FasTrack is a much different concept in track design because it combines the realism of durable plastic with the strength of steel rails.

Basic information about assembling FasTrack and wiring is explained and illustrated in *The Lionel FasTrack Book*. Electrical wiring and additional layout building and operating information are in both *The Big Book of Lionel* and *The Lionel Train Book*.

FasTrack Realism

Lionel fans expect an easy-to-assemble track that functions properly, with everything else a bonus. With FasTrack, the bonus is that it is all very realistic. The ballast looks like loose pieces of rock, the ties like wood, and the simulated spike heads like steel. Surprisingly, the center third rail does not seem to detract from the realism; when FasTrack was introduced the center rail was blackened, but enthusiasts screamed loudly and Lionel repented. Today FasTrack has three shiny steel rails.

FasTrack utilizes an injection-molded plastic base that includes simulated rock ballast roadbed, wood ties, tie plates, and spike heads. The rail is still formed from hollow steel strips with flat metal tabs that fit inside the hollow rails of the adjoining track section. The plastic roadbed has snap interlocks that make an audible click when the track is assembled tightly, and the steel pins in the rails provide both strength and positive electric-current flow.

Before FasTrack became available, if you wanted truly realistic track, you added wood ties and loose ballast to the all-steel track, hopefully with the loose gravel cemented solidly in place. Other brands of track offered more accurate-

Michael Fritschie placed his tabletop FasTrack layout (Chapter 10) in the attic of his home and crafted the scenery.

size ties, but with the challenging prospect of adding that loose ballast and gluing the whole mess to the tabletop. FasTrack combines the realism of loose ballast with the ability to move track to change the layout, or to add or remove sidings without needing to tear the track and glued-down ballast from the tabletop.

FasTrack Layouts

About a dozen basic Lionel track plan configurations have been developed over the past 100 years, most of which are discussed in *The Lionel FasTrack Book* along with the FasTrack geometry. Essentially, Lionel designers were careful and clever enough to produce every size and type of track section the owner could possibly need to create any Lionel layout imaginable, from a 4x8-foot under-bed layout to a 40x80 empire. The layouts can be expanded, modified, and even joined together to create a custom track plan. There are track plans for most of the layouts in this book to serve as suggestions.

FasTrack on a Tabletop

The majority of Lionel FasTrack layouts are simply assembled on the floor, disassembled, and reassembled to suit an owner's whims. You can, however, elevate the layout to a more comfortable height and still rearrange the track anytime you wish.

If you can find the space, I strongly recommend building a permanent table to elevate your Lionel trains about 3 feet from the floor. The trains are even more realistic when viewed from a closer distance, and you can sit in a chair to get the same breathtaking view you would watching a real train from right beside the tracks.

There are a dozen FasTrack layouts on tabletops on these pages, some just bare painted plywood and others with spectacular scenery. A couple are just 6x6 or 5x9, requiring about the same space as a double bed. You can, in fact, assemble a FasTrack layout in as little as 2x8 feet. In some model railroad clubs, members each own their own 2x8 modular piece of the total layout. These clubs meet several times a year in vast halls such as those in convention centers so that a dozen or more members can join their layout modules together into one massive Lionel FasTrack layout, like those in Chapter 7.

You can build a table-like indoor patio deck as shown in Chapter 3, or you can use portable conference tables or one or more table tennis tables. *The Lionel FasTrack Book* contains a lot more table tennis Lionel layouts than does this book. The 5x9 table tennis space is about the minimum size for a Lionel layout, especially if you want the option of changing the track configuration.

Lionel's semi-scale Hudson pulls a string of New York Central cars through one of the rock cuts on Mark Cavaliere's massive FasTrack layout (Chapter 14).

Your FasTrack Model Railroad

Your Lionel model railroad is, first and foremost, yours. Each of us has at least one dream of the perfect Lionel layout. Lionel FasTrack and the clever Legacy Control System make it simple to assemble and operate the layout. If you lack the skill or time, you can have the tables assembled by a professional so that you can concentrate on the track and scenery, or you can hire it all out and just run trains. If you have the space, you can fill a basement or garage. Some, however, prefer to create as simple a layout as possible.

Either way, you can have a layout as exciting as any in this book. Build it all, buy it all, or just buy the parts you'd rather not make yourself. Beware, however, that the plans for these layouts are definitely not blueprints, so you cannot build one for yourself by slavishly following these plans section by section. The simple ovals in this book can be re-created, section for section, but all of the other plans are suggestions, not blueprints. Most of the plans were first created on a computer and then redrawn for more clarity. The layouts that were assembled using these plans definitely did not use

exactly the same number of track sections in every location. The plans were the starting point. When the track was actually laid on the tabletop (or on the elevated supports), a host of slightly longer or shorter track pieces were needed to get everything to fit. You will note that the more complex the plan, the greater number of 1⅜-, 1¾-, 4-, and 5-inch straight-track sections are suggested; they were needed to make the plan work on the computer. When the track was actually laid, it was always changed here and there to make the track line up in the real world. There are no specific places indicated on any of the plans for any of the special track sections like the 6-12020 Uncoupling Track, 6-12029 Accessory Activator, or 6-12054 Operating Track, but any of these can be substituted for any 10-inch standard straight.

Just remember, it is not possible to run trains on a computer screen, so be prepared to fudge a section here or there for a real-world tabletop. Many model railroaders simply design the layout as they lay the track; plans did not exist for Bill Langsdorf's layout in Chapter 13 or Vito Glimco's in Chapter 16, so we have no plans to offer for either of these, not even as suggestions of where they laid their track sections. Because FasTrack offers all the short filler sections you need and a range of curves to fill any gap, these experienced modelers used the trial and error system to build their dream layouts. You can follow a published plan, draw your own on a computer, or just lay down track and run trains. FasTrack makes it that simple.

Who Says You Have To Do It Yourself?

One of the goals of this book is to help you understand that you really can have a dream layout with minimal effort thanks to the simplicity of Lionel FasTrack. Few of us (including myself), however, have the skill required to build a patio deck–style table for a large layout. Fewer of us have the ability to create scenery. I also count myself among those who cannot comprehend the tangle of electrical wiring that a large Lionel layout requires. So I commission someone else to do it!

Hundreds of firms across America build model railroads for customers. These firms will do as little or as much as you wish: They could simply create a track plan and build the benchwork for you. They could install the track and wire it, leaving you to create the scenery, or they could give you a turnkey model railroad where all you do is take the cars and locomotives out of the boxes and put them on the rails. To find a custom-layout builder, start by asking your local dealer. There may be an excellent custom builder within a few miles or hours of your home, and some will even build the layout in your home. Most builders will arrange for delivery, even from coast to coast, but of course the closer the builder is, the cheaper the freight charges.

Before contracting a layout design and construction outfit, check with previous customers to gauge the quality of work. Does it meet your standards? Decide how much you want to contract, how much you are willing to do yourself, and what your budget is. The work will take more hours than you might expect, so it will not be cheap. Shop for a credible builder who can meet both your budget and timeline.

Regardless of whether you do it yourself or contract, you can have the layout of your dreams! Lionel's century of experience has resulted in locomotives and accessories that operate as advertised. FasTrack makes it quick and easy to have reliable and realistic track, and the Lionel Legacy Control System allows you to operate the entire layout from the handheld CAB-2 so that your dream layout operates at the touch of your fingertips.

The crew from the Train Station in Mountain Lakes, New Jersey, assembled Gary Rupert's 8x14-foot layout in his home, including plaster gauze scenery as described in Chapter 6.

CHAPTER 2

Block Wiring, Lionel TrainMaster Command Control, and Lionel Legacy Control System

Lionel trains run with about 18 volts of AC current. The two outer rails carry the negative charge, and the third center rail the positive charge, so the rails are, in effect, the wires that bring both power and control to the trains. A transformer with a variable handle to increase or decrease the amount of

Facing page: The control box for Lumber Loader on Mark Cavaliere's 16x21-foot layout (Chapter 14) is placed right on the tabletop near the accessory. Four black dump bins await logs, coal, or crates, with a FasTrack 6-12054 Operating Track at each bin to activate the log, coal, or boxcar.

Les Kushner and his crew at Main Line Hobbies in East Norriton, Pennsylvania, assembled this layout (Chapter 12) for a customer. A 6-32930 ZW Transformer controls two trains (and provides two adjustable taps for accessory power), and a 6-14198 CW-80 80-watt Transformer controls a third train.

current is used to control the speed of each locomotive. Connect two wires to the track then to the transformer, and you're ready to be the engineer who controls that mighty locomotive. With a few more wires and another transformer, you can control two locomotives or you can opt for the Lionel Legacy Control System or the older TrainMaster system to run up to 99 locomotives with as few as two wire connections to the track.

FasTrack makes it simple to connect the wires to the track. You can use the 6-12016 Terminal Section with wires already installed, or you can simply clip the wires to the metal tabs on the bottom of any standard FasTrack straight track section using a standard 16-gauge female disconnect for 16-14AWG wire, tab size 0.110. 3M's part number is 72F-110-20-P for a package of 100, available through either Mouser or Digi-Key Corporation, or you can simply buy Lionel's 6-12053 Accessory Power Wire. If you are laying FasTrack on a bare tabletop or if the top is covered with felt or fake fur (as shown in *The Lionel FasTrack Book)*, you can run the wires across the top of the table. You can likely find 18-gauge wires to nearly match the color of the tabletop. If you cover the layout with sheets of 1-inch-thick extruded Styrofoam (pink or blue), simply poke holes through the foam with an ice pick or awl, and run the wires between the tabletop and the foam. The best method, however, is to drill through both the Styrofoam and the tabletop, so the wires can be routed beneath the tabletop. If you relocate the switch, light, or accessory, you can always disguise the hole with a piece of green scenic foam.

Operating Two or More Trains at Once

If you want to use Lionel's traditional transformers to run two locomotives, each with independent control, you will need to electrically isolate sections of track to be certain that each locomotive is controlled by only one transformer's speed control. The simple way to achieve independent control for two locomotives is to have separate ovals for each one. You can use two transformers, one for each oval, or buy one of the larger Lionel transformers like the

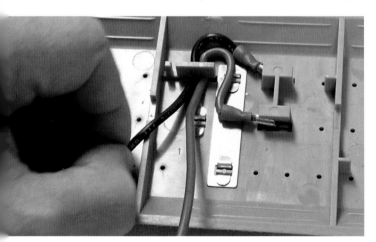

The wires connect to the rails beneath the FasTrack sections. You can either route the wires to the transformer across the tabletop, or drill holes and run the wires beneath the tabletop.

The Lionel TrainMaster CAB-1 Remote (left) and the newer Lionel Legacy Control System CAB-2 Remote (right) are handheld controllers to operate both trains and accessories. The CAB-2 has a display that can be easily programmed to show the locomotive, switch, or accessory (with a brief description).

The crew at the Train Station in Mountain Lakes, New Jersey, assembled this layout for Michael Fritschie (Chapter 10). The nine Remote Switch Controllers are grouped side-by-side with the control box for the Lionel Barrel Loader on the right. The slide switches to the right are made by Atlas to turn lights and blocks on and off.

massive ZW (No. 6-32930 with two 180-watt PowerHouses) with speed controls for two locomotives. Those two ovals can be twisted and contorted into any shape as long as the rails from one oval never touch the rails from the second oval.

»» Block Wiring

To operate two trains at once on the same track, you will need two transformers (or the ZW Transformer) and at least four on-off switches. The track must be divided into train-length or longer electrically isolated blocks. The No. 6-12060 FasTrack Block Section Tracks (and the No. 6-12073 1⅜–inch short track sections) have an insulated center rail to electrically isolate each block. The power can then be connected to each of those blocks with the 6-12016 Terminal Sections. You will also need an on-off (SPDT or Single Pole Double Throw) switch for each block. Wiring a Lionel layout with insulated blocks for operating two or more trains is relatively simple and perfectly logical. *The Lionel FasTrack Book*, Chapter 7 of *The Lionel Train Book*, and *The Big Book of Lionel* have more information on how to wire any FasTrack layout for conventional transformers.

»» Lionel TrainMaster Command Control and Lionel Legacy Control System

Lionel has also developed an electronic digital system that allows you to operate up to 99 locomotives at once without the need for blocks. Lionel's first system was the TrainMaster Command Control (TMCC), introduced in 1995. That system was updated in 2006 to the Lionel Legacy Control System. The Legacy System operates locomotives or accessories from the TMCC. Both utilize a wireless handheld controller similar to some electronic game controllers. A keypad is used to select the locomotive and to control its speed and direction. The keypad can also be used to adjust the rate of acceleration or braking; to blow the whistle, sound the horn, and turn on or off other train sounds; to turn track switches from straight to curve; and even to operate accessories like the Coal Loader.

Both the TMCC and Legacy System utilize similar digital signals that are transmitted from the CAB-1 (TMCC) Remote or the CAB-2 (Legacy System) Remote to receivers inside the locomotives or accessories. The receiver tells the locomotive to speed up or slow down, and how quickly to do so, based on the commands you feed through the CAB-1 or CAB-2. The CAB-1 or CAB-2 can also be used to throw track switches from straight to curve, to uncouple cars, and to turn accessories on or off. For the TMCC or Legacy System to function, you must, of course, have locomotives equipped with TMCC or Legacy System Receivers. Switches and accessories require stationary control devices such as ASC, AMC, and SC-2.

»» Installing TMCC and Legacy System

The new Legacy System and the older TMCC installations are similar.

For TMCC you need the TrainMaster 6-12868 CAB-1 Remote Controller, the 6-12911

TrainMaster Command Base, the 6-14189 TMCC Track Power Controller 300 or the (better) 6-14179 TMCC Track Power Controller 400, and at least one 6-22983 180-watt PowerHouse Power Supply. For more versatility and accessory power choices, the ZW Transformer with its two No. 6-32930 180-watt PowerHouses can be substituted for the 300 or 400 and the single 180-watt PowerHouse Power Supply.

To set up the basic Legacy System, you will need one 990 Legacy Command Set (which includes both a handheld CAB-2 Remote and a combination Command Base and Charger), a TMCC Track Power Controller (300 or 400), and one or more of the 180-watt PowerHouse Power Supply units or the new ZW Transformers.

With either TMCC or the Legacy System, you may need additional 180-watt PowerHouse Power Supply units if you are operating larger locomotives or several locomotives at once. Your dealer can tell you how much power each locomotive requires to help you determine if the 180-watt unit is adequate for your layout.

If you want to operate both TMCC and the Legacy System, the information to connect the two systems is in the Legacy System Wiring Manual.

Lionel Accessories and Automatic Action

We take it as a given today, but operating trains by remote control was truly akin to rocket science in the early 1900s when Lionel was building its heritage. Even today, there's a special thrill when you move the control knob and the locomotive responds with more speed. It's magical when you push a button and the horn wails, the locomotive uncouples from the train, logs are dumped, or the Log Loader's chain hoists into action to lift and reload logs. It is all a wonderful fantasy, with you in complete control of the world you have created.

The Lionel remote control switches have built-in solenoids to throw the switch points. You

Bill Langsdorf operates as many as six trains at once on his layout (Chapter 13) using both Lionel TrainMaster Command Control and the Lionel Legacy Control System, so he needed several of the biggest and most powerful units Lionel offers. The unit with the red knob is the Lionel Legacy CAB-2 resting in its Command Base/Charger, the two silver boxes to the right of it are 6-14179 TMCC Track Power Controllers 400, and the five gray boxes below them are 6-12867 Power Masters with one black box, a TrainMaster 6-12911 Command Base. The four black boxes to the left (with orange and blue Lionel logos) are 6-22983 180-watt PowerHouse Power Supply units, and the three boxes beneath them are the early No. 6-12866 135-watt PowerHouse Power Supply units (no longer produced).

can use the power from the track to power the switches, but the locomotive will slow down a bit each time you throw the switch from straight to curve. Lionel's standard all-steel switches and FasTrack switches offer the option of bypassing the power pickup from the track to connect the switches directly to a separate power source like Lionel's 6-32923 1.8-amp Accessory Transformer. Building lighting, street lights, signals, and of course motor driven accessories like the Log Loader and magnetic cranes also work best with a separate power supply. If you have a

Michael Fritschie uses several Lionel 1531R Controllers (the silver-colored box just beside the locomotive) to actuate signals and crossing gates.

Steve Sherman and his crew from Quality Machine Solutions in Enfield, Connecticut, assembled this FasTrack layout for Mark Cavaliere. The layout is in the final stages of completion, ready for wiring, with each of the 6-12054 Operating Tracks labeled with a dedicated number (which will be indicated on the actuating button), so they can determine which button operates which track section.

Wires for lights, signals, and accessories can be routed through 3/16-inch holes in the tabletop to avoid a cable clutter.

lot of switches, lights, and accessories, you may want to use one of Lionel's ZW Power Supply units so the output voltage can be adjusted to 12-14VAC. There are some helpful tips on wiring on Bill Langsdorf's complex 14x16-foot Legacy layout in Chapter 14.

Lionel offers dozens of signals and crossing gates for use with FasTrack. With Lionel's three-rail track system, you can use one of the rails as a trigger to control signals and to activate warning devices like crossing gatemen and crossing gates. With the Lionel 6-12029 Accessory Activator FasTrack Section, there is no need for special contacts or switches. Just replace two standard straight sections with a set of Accessory Activator Sections, connect the wires as shown in the instructions, and the accessory will be activated each time a train passes.

Lionel offers the 1531R Controller (6-14111) to activate crossing gates or signals using infrared transmissions. The 1531R Controller looks like a track-side maintenance shed, but it houses an infrared detector that can be adjusted for time delay from 0 to 20 seconds. There is no need to attach anything to the track or to use special track sections. Just position the 1531R Controller near the edge of the ballast shoulder and run the wires to the signal or crossing gate and to the power supply. The 1531R is the simplest method of providing control for signals, but on a layout with dozens of signals to be controlled, you may want to alternate between installations of the 1531R Controller and the insulated track sections, especially if you want the signal or crossing warning device to be actuated by trains traveling in either direction.

No matter which methods you decide to utilize, Lionel's range of electronic systems can help you re-create all the action, lighting, and sounds of railroading—automatically or by remote control.

CHAPTER 3

Simple Tables for FasTrack

Lionel has captured the mass of real railroad locomotives and cars and reduced them to fit inside your home. The shape, proportions, and fine details are absolutely authentic; these are real locomotives thundering along on steel rails, just a bit smaller than the ones that deliver automobiles, containers, or passengers. To get the best look at these trains, get your eyes near track level so you can view these incredibly realistic models from the

Facing page: Look carefully and you will see the vertical line that is the joint between each of the tracks on Les Kushner's 12x12-foot layout (Chapter 12). The line between the tabletop sections is disguised with Woodland Scenics' ground foam.

Vito Glimco's Two-Level Line (Chapter 16) is assembled on bench work made from 1x4 boards with 2x4s for the legs, with a 1/2-inch plywood tabletop covered with 2 inches of pink extruded Styrofoam insulation board.

same vantage point you view real trains. Do this by laying the track on the floor and lying down with your head on the floor, or try the easier method: put the tracks and trains on a tabletop.

Tables for Trains

A wide array of options is available for tables to support your Lionel train layout. If you have dedicated space, you can build a permanent table using essentially the same materials and design you would use to build a patio deck. If you know the layout must be taken down occasionally, you can opt for portable tables like fold-up table tennis tables or conference tables.

»» Portability

The area of a portable layout's table is generally divided into rectangles no larger than 30x72 inches. A set of tables that size or smaller are assembled and bolted together with carriage bolts, washers, and nuts. The tabletops are cut to match the table's framework. The sections can be disassembled to make the setup small enough to fit through a standard doorway. If you opt for plaster scenery, the scenery will have to be cut with a saber saw along all the joints and patched when the layout is reassembled. You will also have to remove track sections from the joints between the sections of tabletop. Many layouts are designed so they can be disassembled if they need to be moved, and this holds true for most of the layouts in this book.

»» "Prefab" Portable Tables

A table tennis table is a fine choice for a small Lionel layout. There is just enough room to set up a layout that can handle up to two trains like the one in *The Lionel FasTrack Book*. There's no reason you can't use two, three, or more table tennis tables to create one large table. Arrange three of them in a row for a 5x27-foot layout, in an L-shape for a 9x23 layout, or in a U-shape for a 9x19 layout. You will, however, need to be able to reach the full width of table to assemble the tracks and to re-rail any derailed trains. Table tennis tables are not sturdy enough for you to crawl or walk on, so you need at least 2½ feet of access around the entire perimeter of the layout. One

The track-leading upper level on Gary Rupert's 8x14-foot layout (Chapter 11), is supported by half of the Lionel 6-12037 Graduated Trestle Set.

end of a table tennis table can be against the wall as long as you have 2½ feet of access on the other three sides. This will keep your reach at a 2½–foot maximum on a 5-foot table width.

You can also assemble a Lionel layout on two or more conference tables. Conference tables are available in a wide range of sizes, but the largest manageable ones are 2½x6 or 2½x8. You will need at least two to create a 5x6 or 5x8 area. You can use two or three side-by-side pairs of conference tables to create a tabletop from 5x12 to as long as 5x24. The folding legs for these tables are available separately, and you can use them to assemble your own table from ½-inch plywood with 1x2-inch braces along the sides.

»» Custom-Built Tables

Any general carpenter can assemble the table for you, either in your home or in their shop. Think of this project as ordering a portable patio deck!

Remember, though, to be sure to discuss with the builder your table's specs and the aspect of moving the layout. Many builders create the entire layout and scenery in their shop then disassemble it for the move into your house. The layout is then reassembled and the seams detailed between individual tables at your home. It's best to have a conversation about portability *before* you have your new layout designed and constructed.

»» Permanent Tables

If you have the space for a large Lionel layout you can construct a permanent table for the trains. Most Lionel layouts are built on tables with 2x4-inch legs spaced every 4 feet, with a patio deck framework of 1x4-inch lumber with joists spaced 2 feet apart. All of the permanent layouts in this book have these types of supports for the tabletop.

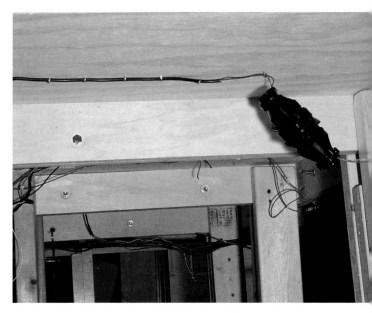

Custom Train Layouts assembled the benchwork for Mark Cavaliere's 16x21-foot Appalachian Empire (Chapter 14), so the layout can be disassembled into 30x72-inch sections and moved if necessary.

There is no standard height for a Lionel layout. Some prefer the traditional 30-inch table height, others elevate the tabletop just 2 feet so younger children can see the trains, and others prefer layouts as high as 4½ feet so they can view their trains at eye level without having to sit or kneel.

Tabletops

HO-scale model railroaders usually do not install a tabletop. They cut ½-inch plywood to match the locations of the track and elevate the plywood on risers above the open benchwork (like Mark Cavaliere's layout in Chapter 14). You can, of course, do that with Lionel, but you lose the option of relocating the track. Most Lionel layouts are assembled on a flat tabletop so the track can be relocated. That's one of the advantages of FasTrack—it's so easy to disassemble and reassemble that you can make changes whenever you desire.

Most model railroaders choose ½-inch plywood rather than particleboard or

The 1-inch layer of Styrofoam is cut away so the 2x6-inch risers can be screwed directly to the plywood tabletop on Mark Cavaliere's 16x21-foot layout (Chapter 14).

The 2x6-inch risers are attached with simple steel angle brackets and woodscrews on Bill Langsdorf's 14x16-foot Legacy layout (Chapter 13).

MDF board for the tabletop. If you use the less-expensive boards, they must be supported by joints spaced to form egg crate–style boxes no larger than 24x24 inches, or the board will sag. Opt for plywood. You can use the less-expensive BC grade or even rough, outdoor plywood.

A bare plywood, particleboard, or MDF board tabletop amplifies the sound of the trains rumbling down the track to the point of annoyance. I strongly recommend that you cover a bare-wood tabletop with a 1- or 2-inch-thick layer of blue or pink extruded polystyrene like Dow Corning's blue Styrofoam. The white bead board (expanded polystyrene) is too soft for this use. The 1- or 2-inch thickness will also provide the option of cutting into the Styrofoam to make lakes or streams below track level, as shown in Chapter 5.

Two-Level Layouts

You may want an elevated track just for the thrill of watching one train pass over another or to provide a second level for a town or industrial area, thus squeezing in more operation in a given area. You'll see examples of both types of upper-level tracks on the layouts shown in later chapters.

Lionel provides a simple method of creating a second level with the 6-12037 Graduated Trestle Set to gently ramp up the track from tabletop to an elevation of 5½ inches. The trestles are re-creations of the wood piers (or "bents," in railroad terms) of real railroad trestles with bases that can be screwed to the tabletop using 1½-inch-long wood screws. The tops of the trestle bents are designed to hold the metal clips that retain the edges of FasTrack. Lionel also offers the 6-12038 Elevated Trestle Set with enough bents to support the track at 5½ inches for about 4 feet of track. Lionel also offers

The side-by-side 2x4 vertical supports are on opposite sides of the joints between two of the sections of Mark Cavaliere's layout (Chapter 14) to allow the layout to be disassembled.

The upper-level tracks on Gary Rupert's layout (Chapter 11) are supported by vertical 1x4s with 1x6s to support the tracks.

a variety of piers to support the elevated tracks, including the 6-12744 Rock Piers.

You can alternatively use ½-inch plywood and the 1-inch extruded Styrofoam to support elevated tracks. The plywood can be supported above the tabletop with 5½-inch-long 1x6 boards placed every 18 to 24 inches. The 1x6 boards can be attached to the tabletop with 2-inch wood screws angled or toe-nailed to the tabletop, or with simple steel angle braces. Use the Graduated Trestle Set to get the lower-level track to and from the upper level. The uphill and downhill grades should never be any steeper than a 5½-inch rise per 100 inches of track, which is the grade that results from the Graduated Trestle Set.

The upper level can cover as much as half of the layout, as it does on Bill Langsdorf's 14x16-foot Legacy layout in Chapter 13. Plans on page 137 of *The Lionel FasTrack Book* illustrate how Bill used 2x8 and 4x8 sheets of plywood to assemble his layout. Each of those 2x8 and 4x8 sections is a separate framed layout table with sections clamped together by carriage bolts, washers, and nuts so that he can disassemble the layout. All of the surfaces are covered with at least one 1-inch layer of pink extruded Styrofoam.

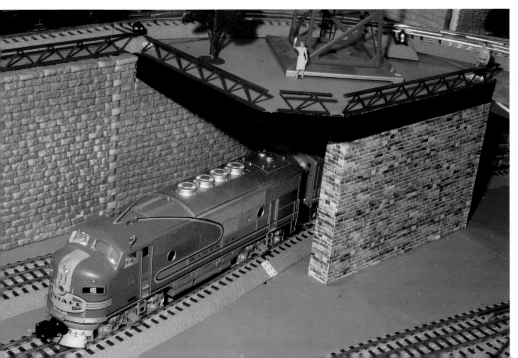

Bill Langsdorf wrapped some of the 1x6 vertical support boards with stone-pattern paper to create some simple realism on this layout (Chapter 13).

CHAPTER 4

Bridges

Mountains and rivers were a challenge to actual railroads and had to be surmounted in the most efficient way. In the earliest days of railroad construction, bridges were built so the railroads could cross rivers rather than rely on ferries. On a Lionel layout, bridges are easy to install and provide instant scenery. Slip a bridge beneath the track and it implies a river, a valley, hills, and more.

Facing page: A set of Lionel 6-12038 Elevated Trestle Set Bents support the 24-inch Truss Bridge and the upper-level track on Vito Glimco's layout (Chapter 16).

These two Lionel deck girder bridges and truss bridge were painted dark gray and weathered with a dry brush of lighter gray by the Custom Model Train Layouts builders on Mark Cavaliere's layout (Chapter 14).

Lionel Bridge Options

Lionel offers bridges galore. Lionel design engineers have always recognized that a Lionel layout is likely to be assembled on a flat floor or a solid tabletop. Few Lionel model railroaders have built their Lionel layouts with the option of a valley lower than tracks for the bridge to span. Nearly all of the Lionel bridges are therefore designed to slip between the track and the tabletop. If the bridge must be elevated an inch or two, the supports to elevate the track for that short height are included with the bridge.

»» Plate Girder Bridges

Lionel's most popular bridge is the simple replica of the riveted-steel-plate girder bridge. The solid plate cast-metal rounded-corner 314 Girder Bridge was first produced in 1940 and has been a staple of Lionel's series of

Vito Glimco's layout (Chapter 16) has two Lionel Deck Girder Bridges—a No. 270 Deck Truss Bridge and 10-inch Short Extension Bridge.

You can simulate a truss bridge with simple 1/4x1/2-inch balsa or bass wood strips with 1/8x3/8-inch square vertical and cross braces like this one on Les Kushner's layout (Chapter 12).

bridges ever since. A 214 Plate Girder Bridge plastic model with the ends at 45-degree angles supplemented the cast-metal bridge in 1953.

»» Truss Bridges

Lionel's first bridge was the open-top red 270 Truss Bridge introduced in 1931, which has been reproduced for today's layouts.

The most common Lionel Truss Bridge is a 24-inch-long closed-top steel truss. The bridge was first produced in stamped steel, and Lionel has since offered reproductions of that bridge. In 1958 Lionel introduced the plastic replica of it, the Trestle Bridge. The bridge has been offered in two styles, with an arched top and with the top parallel to the bottom. All have stamped-steel bases for strength.

A very toy-like, all-plastic 10-inch Short Extension Bridge version of the Arched-Top Truss Bridge is available to simply rest beside the ends of the ties.

»» Wood Trestles

You can create a realistic replica of the old wooden trestles by using three of the 5½-inch-tall bents from the Lionel 6-12038 Elevated Trestle Set for every 10 inches of track. Vito Glimco used a series of these trestle bents to support the upper-level track on his layout in Chapter 16. Your hobby dealer can also order kits with pre-assembled wood bents up to 17 inches tall to build trestles with real wood components, like the Scenic Express Wood Trestle Bridge System. Doug

The track leading onto the plaster cloth mountain on Gary Ruppert's layout (Chapter 11) is supported by 5 1/2-inch-tall bents from the Lionel 6-12038 Elevated Trestle Set.

Waller has crafted a curved wood trestle for his FasTrack layout in Chapter 15.

»» Bridges for Curves

There are a lot of curves on a Lionel layout. Unfortunately, the only Lionel bridges that will fit on a curve are the individual bents or supports in the No. 6-12037 Graduated Trestle Set. Use some of the shortest of these bents to simulate bridge supports for shorter bridges, spacing the bents about 3 inches apart.

If the upper-level track is supported on ½-inch plywood and 1-inch Styrofoam, cut the plywood and Styrofoam to match the width of the FasTrack roadbed. Custom Model Train Layouts devised a clever method of simulating cast-concrete deck bridges that is especially useful on curves. The crew uses a double-wide blade to cut ¹⁄₁₆-inch wide and

⅛-inch deep notches every ½ inch, in ¼x2-inch wood strips. The notches look like seams in concrete and allow the strips to be flexible enough to bend around curves. The strips are then cemented to the sides of plywood upper-level track supports. The strips are painted medium gray and dry brushed with a darker gray to create the appearance of cast concrete. There are several of them on Mark Cavaliere's layout in Chapter 14.

»» Bridges for Ships

When the railroad crosses a river or canal that is used by taller ships, the railroad must either build an embankment high enough so the bridge will clear the tops of the tallest ships, or provide a means of moving the bridge so the tall ships can pass. There are several styles of full-size bridges that move aside to allow

Doug Waller used 1/4-inch-square basswood strips for the vertical beams and 1/8x3/16-inch basswood strips for the braces on the wood trestle for his layout (Chapter 15).

the taller ships to pass, including the swing-up, or bascule bridge; the lift bridge; and the swing bridge. Lionel has re-created them all.

»» The Lionel Hell Gate Bridge

The Hell Gate Bridge was opened in 1917 in Upper Manhattan to allow northeastern New England rail traffic to reach New York City more efficiently. The bridge is near the confluence of the East and Hudson rivers, and the turbulent waters were given the name Hell

Gate. The steel arch spanned 977 feet—that's about 20 feet when reduced to O scale. Lionel re-created a much-foreshortened stamped-steel version of the Hell Gate Bridge in 1928. The bridge was, however, a massive 30-inch-long model. Lionel's model was considered the engineering marvel of toys in the 1930s and 1940s. Lionel has reintroduced several color variations of the Hell Gate Bridge over the past 10 years as part of the Lionel Classic series.

The Lionel Classics reproduction of the 1928 stamped-steel Hell Gate Bridge on Bill Langsdorf's FasTrack layout (Chapter 13).

»» Styrofoam Bridges

If you cover your tabletop with a 1- or 2-inch layer of blue or pink Styrofoam, you can carve valleys for your bridges to span into the Styrofoam. If the valleys you create are narrow enough, you may not need a bridge. If you create scenery for your FasTrack layout like that described in Chapter 5, the FasTrack roadbed itself can be enough to simulate a short bridge. The real railroads would use a steel or concrete pipe, but those are not always visible—so just let the track hang there, suggesting there is a steel or concrete pipe hidden in the shadows.

»» Bridge Abutments

In the real world, the ends of the bridge must be supported on piers substantial enough to carry the weight of several locomotives. Lionel has offered a variety of piers to support the elevated tracks, including the 6-12744 Rock Piers as well as some earlier plastic replicas of cut-stone piers. Some modelers use the simulated-wood trestle bents from the 6-12038 Elevated Trestle Set to support the deck girder or steel truss bridges. If you are building an upper level to cross over the tracks onto the lower level, the bridge needs to be elevated about 5 inches or more above the rails of the lower level. Lionel Rock Piers and other abutments are designed to provide that overhead clearance.

If you have elevated the upper level on ½-inch plywood with 2x4-foot vertical supports, you can disguise the 2x4 verticals as bridge abutments simply by painting them. The crew from Custom Model Train Layouts paints the abutments dark gray and dry brushes

Notched 1/4x2-inch wood trim strips with 1/8-inch-deep notches can be cemented to both sides of an upper-level track to simulate a cast-concrete bridge.

With a 1-inch or thicker Styrofoam tabletop cover, you can cut small streams into the Styrofoam and simply suspend the track above the stream, as shown in Chapter 5.

streaks of lighter gray to simulate concrete, like on Mark Cavaliere's layout in Chapter 14. The shop used the same technique to highlight rivet detail on the girder and truss bridges.

You can match the look of stone retaining walls or bridge abutments on 1x6 or 2x6 vertical supports with the Plastruct 91587, 7x12-inch sheets of 0.020-inch thick styrene that are embossed and painted to simulate dressed stone block in ¼8 scale. Cut the sheets with a scissors or a knife to fit the sides of a 1x6 or 2x6 vertical bridge support. Cement the sheets to the wood with Shoe GOO or water-based contact cement. Touch-up the edges with a dark-gray felt-tip pen. Scenic Express offers a No. NH57720 package of six embossed 5x22x½-inch cards with photographic reproduction of granite stone, dolomite, basalt block, red block, quarry stone, and sandstone that can also be used to wrap vertical supports for more realism.

Weathering Bridges by Dry Brushing

You can increase the realism of any of Lionel's plastic bridges and their metal deck girder bridges by painting the bridge dark gray. When the paint dries, pour some medium-gray latex paint in a shallow pan. Dip just the tip of a ¼-inch-wide, flat paint brush into light gray paint, then barely touch the brush to the surface of the model so the lighter gray touches on the raised details, like rivets and seams. It's a technique that professional builders from Custom Model Train Layouts used on the bridges and rock faces of the scenery for Mark Cavaliere's layout in Chapter 14.

Bill Langsdorf simply painted the edges of the plywood support surface for the upper level black and the upper layer of 1-inch Styrofoam green for this layout (Chapter 13). The vertical surfaces are covered with embossed stone sheet.

Custom Model Train Layouts builders used notched 1/4x2-inch wood strips to simulate concrete bridge girders on Mark Cavaliere's layout (Chapter 14).

CHAPTER 5

Creating Mountains, Valleys, Streams, and Lakes

The vision of a mile-long train snaking its way through the hills and over the rivers is surprisingly simple to create with your Lionel FasTrack. Model railroaders have been experimenting with different techniques and materials to shape mountains, grow weeds and trees, and fill rivers for over 100 years. Some

modern materials have emerged that minimize the mess and virtually guarantee successful scenes.

Permanent Scenery

Before you cover your entire layout with replicas of the Rocky Mountains, decide if you really want to keep that exact track location. One of the joys of Lionel trains is that it is so easy to change the track to provide a different route, or to add sidings or reverse loops. If you have covered the tabletop with scenery right up to the edges of the track, you will have to chip away the scenery to relocate the tracks. There's information on how to create truly portable scenery from

fake fur and flexible and portable rock walls in *The Lionel FasTrack Book*.

There is a compromise that lets you enjoy the best of both worlds: Dedicate a portion of your layout table to be left flat and without scenery. That can be all but one corner with mountains, like Vito Glimco's layout in Chapter 16, or just a couple of 4-foot-square corners where you install and rearrange operating

continued on page 38

Facing page: The cliff faces constructed by the Custom Train Layouts crew for Mark Cavaliere's layout (Chapter 14) were carved from blue extruded Styrofoam painted with interior latex wall paint and dry brushed to bring out the textures and shapes.

The tabletop on Les Kushner's layout (Chapter 12) was covered with a 2-inch layer of pink extruded Styrofoam to support the lower-level track. The middle-level track is supported on three more layers of 2-inch pink extruded Styrofoam, and the upper-level track is supported by four more layers of 2-inch Styrofoam. The multiple layers of Styrofoam are cut with a hot knife to expose the track on the lower level, and the walls of the cuts are painted dark gray, like the lower-level track in the upper-left.

Even a layout on a table tennis tabletop can have permanent scenery. Cover the table with a 1-inch or 2-inch layer of pink or blue extruded Styrofoam, with additional layers for mountains.

I wanted a streambed, so I added a 2-inch layer of blue Styrofoam between the 1-inch layer and the track.

Mark the edges of the FasTrack roadbed on the Styrofoam and remove the track.

Use a hacksaw blade or a hot-wire cutter to carve the angled faces of the valley into the Styrofoam.

I used some of the leftover scraps of Styrofoam to fill the edges of this shallow valley. The track could be supported with one of the shortest piers from the Lionel 6-12037 Graduated Trestle Set.

Seven 2-inch layers of blue Styrofoam shape this mountain on Mark Cavaliere's layout (Chapter 14). The opening will be filled with a removable 2x3-foot section of mountain to provide an access hatch for maintenance.

Continued from page 35
industrial accessories the like the Lionel Log Loader, Coal Elevator, or Magnetic Crane.

If you are creating scenery beside the tracks, remember to allow enough room to be certain that the locomotives and longest cars do not sideswipe the mountain, tunnel, tree, action accessory, or structure. Test run the longest cars or locomotives through any new sections of scenery so you can make modifications before a derailment.

Scenery from Styrofoam

The common blue or pink Dow Corning extruded Styrofoam insulation board has become the staple for model railroad layout scenery. Start with a 1- or 2-inch layer over the entire tabletop. The Styrofoam will dampen the rumble from the plywood tabletop so you hear more metal wheels clacking over rail joints and less vibrating plywood. That layer of Styrofoam also provides the space

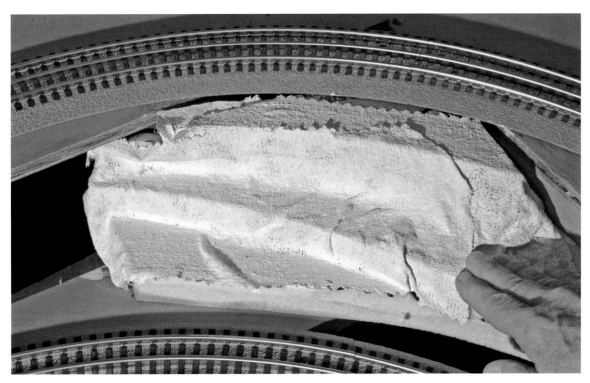

The carved Styrofoam will be much easier to paint and texture if you cover it with a layer of plaster. You can use Woodland Scenics Plaster Cloth and simply shape it over the carved Styrofoam.

Les Kushner used plaster dissolved in water colored with Rit Dye to cover the exposed-rock walls of his cut.

Bill Langsdorf holds the retaining walls to the carved Styrofoam scenery with map pins on his layout (Chapter 13). The angled wall is a Scenic Express No. FL-6190 "Pennsy" Retaining Wing Set.

you need to create shallow valleys, so your railroad's bridges really do span a valley rather than just resting on the tabletop.

I wanted a 2-inch-deep valley, so I elevated a portion of the track on a second layer of 2-inch Styrofoam, placed on top of the 1-inch layer that covered the plywood tabletop. For deeper valleys, simply insert additional 2-inch layers of Styrofoam beneath the track.

The Styrofoam can be glued with Liquid Nails Project & Foamboard Adhesive LN 604 or similar cements that will not attack the Styrofoam. Woodland Scenics' Low Temp Foam Glue Gun ST1445 with matching glue sticks can be used for faster bonds. Normal "white" glue will not dry in the closed space between the plywood tabletop and the Styrofoam covering.

»» Carving Styrofoam Scenery

Mark the edges of the FasTrack roadbed with a pencil so you don't cut too close to the tracks. Carve the Styrofoam with a hacksaw blade, holding the blade with either a gloved hand or mounting it in one of the handles that grip just one end of the blade. The Styrofoam is soft, so it only takes a little pressure on the hacksaw blade. You can also carve the Styrofoam with a hot-wire cutter like the Tippi Hot-Wire Foam Cutter, but be sure to work in a well-ventilated area, because the melted Styrofoam produces a noxious gas. Take your time to be sure you have the blade angled just the way you want it. If you make a mistake and cut too deep, you can glue the incorrectly cut piece back in place. The sawing will produce a nearly weightless powder that clings to everything. Keep a vacuum cleaner with a flexible vacuum hose near the cutting area, with the vacuum turned on to collect the powder before it spreads around the room.

The rock faces on Les Kushner's layout in Chapter 12 and on Mark Cavaliere's layout in Chapter 14 are carved directly into the foam before coating the foam with a layer of pre-colored plaster. You want the

This curved retaining wall on Mark Cavaliere's layout (Chapter 14) was mounted on a separate 1-inch strip of blue Styrofoam, so the wall could be removed for access to the track wiring. The wall is a connected set of four flexible Scenic Express FL-8150 "Pennsy" Flexi-Walls.

The mountain on Vito Glimco's layout (Chapter 16) occupies only a small portion of the flat tabletop to give him the option of relocating the tracks on most of the layout. The Scenic Express MM0150 Tunnel Portal is similar to these two portals.

Bill Langsdorf used the Scenic Express flexible FL-7151 "Howard Street" Flexi-Walls with interlocking edges for the sides and top of this tunnel portal.

Les Kushner used the No. 4188 Evergreen 0.040-inch thick V-groove styrene sheet and 0.188x0.188-inch strips to build this two-level tunnel portal to match the general shape and style of the Scenic Express No. FL6195 Timber Frame Portal.

rock to look crude, so use anything that's handy. Les used a crowbar, chisel, old steak knives, surform rasp, and barbeque brushes to scrape and pry against the surface.

»» Styrofoam Mountains

Most of us dream of a model railroad with spectacular scenery that includes deep chasms and ceiling-high mountains. Mark Cavaliere's 16x21 FasTrack layout in Chapter 14 has that kind of breathtakingly realistic scenery. There is a downside to such scenery, however: You cannot relocate most of the tracks without tearing out much of the scenery and starting over. On Mark's layout, there are two large flat areas for the main yard and an industrial park where the sidings can be relocated without disturbing the scenery. Since the ballast is built into FasTrack, relocating track is easy, and you can simply add more

ground-foam ground cover to complete the surface, as shown in Chapter 5.

To make mountains with Styrofoam, simply stack 2-inch sheets in pyramid fashion. Each 2-inch layer should be at least 2 inches smaller all around than the next lower layer to keep the slope reasonably realistic. More gentle slopes will have each layer of 2-inch Styrofoam at least 4 inches smaller than the next lowest layer. You can vary the slopes from very gentle to steep as necessary. The crew from Custom Train Layouts created the mountain on Mark Cavaliere's layout with a 2x3-foot lift-out center section (which is removed in the photos) to provide an access hatch in the center of the layout. The mountain rises on six layers of 2-inch Styrofoam, each layer about 2 inches smaller than the one below it. The crew stacked a pyramid of the six layers of Styrofoam and carved the gentle slopes with a hacksaw blade.

Les Kushner carved the pink Styrofoam into rough rock shapes, covered it with plaster ,and left it in that rough state to re-create a blasted-rock tunnel portal.

Texturing the Earth's Surface

The carved Styrofoam is far too rough to resemble dirt slopes, unlike most rock textures. Smooth the surface with a layer of plaster. You can use common wall plaster, or plaster-impregnated 12x12 Woodland Scenics Plaster Cloth or Scenic Express Plaster Wrap. Simply dip the plaster-impregnated gauze in water and drape the sodden gauze over the Styrofoam scenery. I advise you to color the water with black or dark brown Rit Dye so the plaster isn't stark white. Though you might paint and texture the surface, any accidental chips or areas you fail to cover won't be stark-white plaster if you tint the water.

Realistic Rock Faces

Mountains in Minutes Flexrock is available in three 7x16-inch foam-rubber textures: 501 Rock Canyon, 502 Rock Embankment, and 503 Rock Gorge. Scenic Express also has a range of flexible walls and rock faces. You can bend the foam-rubber rocks to more or less conform to the shape of the carved-Styrofoam slopes and attach the flexible rocks to the plaster or to the blue Styrofoam with Liquid Nails Project & Foamboard Adhesive LN 604, or use Woodland Scenics' Low Temp Foam Glue Gun ST1445. These flexible rocks are pre-colored, so protect the rock face with taped-on clear plastic while you finish the scenery.

With care, you can carve smooth rock faces directly into the Styrofoam like that on Mark Cavaliere's layout in Chapter 14. The professional builders from Custom Model Train Layouts crafted some spectacular rock faces directly into the Styrofoam, then painted them with latex wall paint

Lionel's series of animated playground and park scenes, like this 6-24137 "Mr. Spiff and Puddles" on Michael Fritschie's layout (Chapter 10), look more realistic if textured with the same ground foam as the surrounding grass.

and highlighted the textures with the dry-brushing techniques described in Chapter 4.

Woodland Scenics and Scenic Express offer a variety of latex rubber molds that you can use to cast your own rocks with plaster of Paris. To install these rocks, slap the mold against the scenery with the still-wet plaster inside and hold it there for a minute until plaster hardens; then immediately remove the mold so the plaster does not tear the flexible mold. When dry, paint the rock to match the real-world area you are re-creating and apply a stain of 1 part burned umber acrylic paint to 10 parts water. The stain will accent the crevices in the rocks. You can dry brush some of the rock faces with light gray acrylic paint to re-create the variegated colors of real rock.

Retaining Walls

Space is always tight on a tabletop layout, so there is seldom room for the gentle slopes of real mountains. Even rough-stone cliffs can use more space than available. There are, however, a variety of simulated stone retaining walls that require less than ½ inch of space. Check out the flexible urethane products cemented to the sides of the plywood upper-level supports on Mark Cavaliere's layout in Chapter 14, which make great retaining walls. Most are the "Pennsy" Flexi-Wall FL9150 from Scenic Express.

Tunnels

Where there's a mountain, there's an excuse, at least, for a tunnel on a Lionel layout. Even on a relatively flat layout you can justify installing

Doug Waller created a few tiny scenic mounds by draping plaster cloth over small wads of newspaper. He colored the mounds and placed them on the tabletop, then surrounded them with a 1/4-inch-thick layer of loose ballast. He flooded the area with a mixture of equal parts artist's matte medium and water to secure the loose ballast. If the track needs be moved, the ballast will easily pry loose with a spatula.

a tunnel portal, rather than a bridge, where the lower-level track dives beneath the upper level.

Dozens of replicas of cast concrete, stone, and wood tunnel portals are available for your Lionel FasTrack layout. Lionel No. 6-12896 is a plastic replica of a cast concrete tunnel portal. Chooch and Scenic Express have a variety of stone, cast concrete, and wood tunnel portals for both single and double track. If you are casting rocks for cliffs on your mountain, you can consider creating your own tunnel portal. If the mountain was solid rock, railroads sometimes just blasted the tunnel through

rock, so the portal was just rough stone. Scenic Express offers an FL6550 Blasted Rock Portal for single-track layouts.

You can buy ready-made white expanded polystyrene (bead board) mountains, complete with two tunnel portals from Life-Like. You could texture the toy-like mountain using the techniques in this chapter to improve its realism.

Real Dirt and Foam Grass Textures
The most realistic dirt is real dirt. Test any dirt you want to use with a magnet to determine if there are iron particles and,

Woodland Scenics, Scenic Express, and Life-Like offer ground foam in several sizes and dozens of colors. Coat the scenery surface with artist's matte medium then sprinkle the foam on the still-wet matte medium for a realistic effect.

Sift real dirt through a tea strainer and sprinkle it on the artist's matte medium–coated surface to simulate dirt.

Dip small pebbles in undiluted artist's matte medium and cement them to the textured surface.

Put just a thin layer of plaster cloth over the shaped Styrofoam so the trees can simply be pushed into the surface. Punch a hole with an ice pick or awl, and shove the trunk of the tree into the hole.

if so, find another source of dirt. Use a tea strainer to sift the dirt to remove the larger particles. Grass and weeds can be simulated with the ground foam rubber from Woodland Scenics or Scenic Express.

Before you sprinkle dirt or ground foam, cover the surface with undiluted artist's matte medium—cover only about a square foot or so at a time, so the matte medium doesn't dry before you can sprinkle on the sifted dirt or ground foam. If you are covering larger areas, you can use the clear matte faux finish latex wall paint, which is nearly identical to matte medium but only a fraction of the price. When you are completely satisfied with the surfaces,

spray on a mixture of one part matte medium to four parts water, plus a drop or two of dishwashing detergent. Completely flood the area so it looks milky white. This final step will minimize the chances that loose texture particles find their way into the locomotives, cars, switches, or action accessories.

Trees and Bushes

Ready-built deciduous trees and coniferous trees are available from Woodland Scenics, Scenic Express, Pola, Model Power, Life-Like, and Noch. For a Lionel layout, use trees that are 5- to 14-inches tall. Each tree has a large plastic base that allows

Les Kushner painted the bottom of this lake blue on the 5x9-foot layout (Chapter 12). One or two layers of decoupage resin will be poured over the area to create the wet look, and the blue will add depth.

the tree to be freestanding on a flat tabletop. You can remove the base and punch a hole in the plaster or Styrofoam to "plant" the trees in permanent scenery.

Water

It is usually easier to add the water to the scenery than to try to build the scenery around the water. If you want "portable" water, I recommend clear plastic sheets of simulated-ripple water from Faller (170791), Kibri (4126), or Noch (60850 and 60851). As an alternative, crumpled-up aluminum foil, flattened to level some of the gentle wrinkles, is surprisingly realistic.

If you have permanent scenery, you can use one of the pourable-water products to simulate water. For streams or ponds just an inch or two wide, you can simply pour in some gloss medium. You may need to temporarily tilt the scenery to bring it level when using any of these pour-in products to keep the fluid from running right off the table. For larger streams or lakes, use decoupage casting resin colored with a few drops of olive drab Rit Dye. Scenic Express and Woodland Scenics have special pour-in products and kits to create waterfalls and rapids. All of these material look like water, especially when contrasted with the dirt and foam-textured ground scenery that surrounds them.

Pour the mixture of decoupage resin and catalyst over the hollow that will be the bottom of the stream or pond.

The hardened decoupage resin looks exactly like real water.

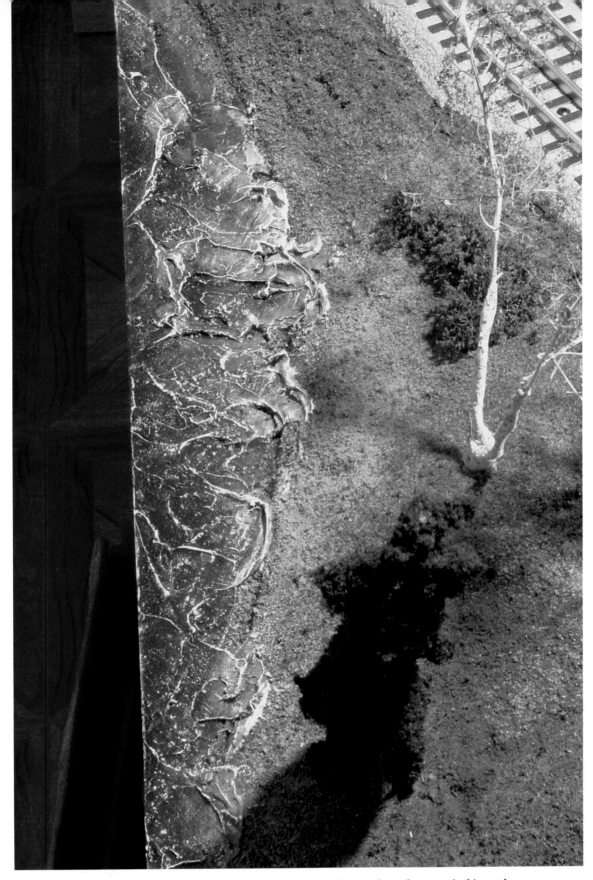

The crew at Custom Train Layouts used the paste-like artist's gel medium to shape the waves in this seashore scene on Mark Cavaliere's layout (Chapter 14). The waves were painted dark blue with the crests dry brushed with flecks of white to simulate white caps.

CHAPTER 6

The City as Scenery

There is never enough room on even the largest Lionel layout for all the spectacular scenery we want to create. Given the tight spaces, consider using vertical scenery, which doesn't use as much valuable layout space. Though real railroad trains spend the majority of their journeys in the country, they pass through cities along the way, making vertical city structures a great scenery choice.

The Lionelville series of buildings has included a complete range of houses, several small businesses, an array of animated playground and park accessories, and a variety of Lionelville People Packs. Lionel has also offered the Lionel Midtown Hobby Shop building, with full interior lighting and an all-skylight roof so you could see the three operating Lionel layouts inside, complete with scenery and bridges. In 2003, a nearly identical building was offered but as a Ford automobile dealership with salesman, buyers, and automobiles on rotating stands. Lionel also offered a stamped-steel Lionel Factory in 1999 that was similar to Lionel's early Irvington, New Jersey, factory. The Lionel Coal Loader, Log Loader, and Magnetic and Intermodal Cranes are all appropriate for city industrial scenes.

Creating a City

While there may not be room for a scale model city, there can be enough space for a small town. Place a few select structures strategically, however, and you'll effectively suggest a much larger city just beyond. Consider houses to be an important part of the fringes of the major city that your railroad serves.

Facing page: The brick Hotel Building on the left is an Ameri-Towne No. 442. The Hotel Building is actually six freestanding buildings placed wall to wall, six panels wide and just one panel deep. The Drug Store on the right was assembled with six No. 77 Ameri-Towne Savings & Loan fronts. The Rexall Drug sign is No. 66812 from Light Works by Miller Engineering.

>>> Build a City with Blocks

There have been very few downtown city buildings in O scale, because there is no way of predicting how large a structure you might need. There are, however, two excellent modular wall systems that, in effect, allow you to construct any size building, like you might stack a child's building blocks. With these wall units, you assemble each of the four walls—building-block style—join the four walls, then provide some interior bracing and a roof.

The Design Preservation Models O Scale Modular System is a complete series of injection-molded plastic wall sections. Each section is $4\frac{1}{8}$ inches wide and $3\frac{1}{16}$ inches tall, and all are interchangeable. They occasionally offer a complete building kit, but the system allows you to build virtually any size structure, from a 4-inch-square shop to a ten-story hotel.

The $4\frac{1}{8}$-inch-wide by $3\frac{1}{16}$-inch-tall wall sections include:

- 90101 Street/Dock Level Arched Entry
- 90102 Arched Window
- 90103 Blank Wall
- 90104 Street/Dock Level Rectangular Entry
- 90105 Rectangular Window
- 90106 Double Rectangular Window
- 90107 Street/Dock Level Freight Door
- 90108 Dock Riser (to elevate a building to the freight-car floor level for industry models)

Design Preservation also offers a $4\frac{1}{4}$-inch-wide, two-story brick store, No. 801 Birdies Tavern, which can be combined with modular walls to create larger downtown structures.

>>> The Ameri-Towne Modular Wall System

Ameri-Towne offers an injection-molded plastic modular wall system as well as complete building kits. The kits make it somewhat easier to create a complete building, because

With the Ameri-Towne modular wall system, use a cabinetmaker's file to smooth the vertical joining surfaces of the walls.

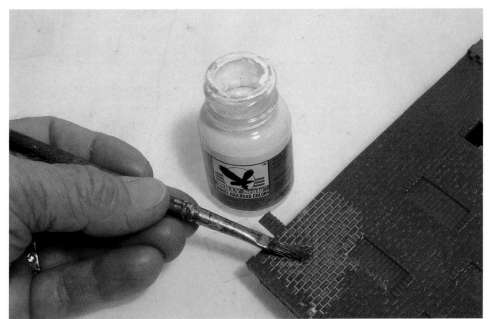

The mortar lines can be accented with a wash of five parts thinner to one part paint. The dilute color will settle into the seams to produce the effect of mortar around every brick.

they include details like the roof, sidewalk, lintel caps for the top story, and printed-paper interior scenes. The building kits are designed to be expanded, either by joining with modular wall panels from additional Ameri-Towne kits or by purchasing individual front walls or rear walls. Each of the Ameri-Towne wall section is 6 inches wide and 4 inches high. The front walls are about ¼ inch thick to provide the depth needed for brick and stone lintels and inset doorways and windows. All of the larger buildings on Mike Hill's 6x6-foot city layout later in this chapter were assembled from Ameri-Towne kits by Doug Waller at Main Line Hobbies in East Norriton, Pennsylvania.

Assembling a City

The Ameri-Towne and Design Preservation kits must be assembled from at least five flat pieces of injection-molded styrene plastic. Each of the four walls must be joined at the vertical corners. Use a large, flat file like a cabinetmaker's to smooth the adjoining edges so the cement can hold more readily. Testors Liquid Plastic Cement works well to cement the seams. Apply the cement to both surfaces, then hold the joining faces together and rub them up and down with some pressure to help soften the plastic. Assemble all four walls and wrap the structure around the top, middle, and bottom with masking tape to hold the joints tight while the cement dries overnight.

»» Assembling Larger City Blocks

If you are going to join two or more walls side-by-side, you need to slice off the 45-degree mitered corners of the adjoining walls. Hobby dealers sell a Mascot No. 5 Knife Handle and a No. 102 Razor-Saw Blade that work well for cutting the relatively soft styrene plastic. Use the saw to cut off just the angled edge, and finish the cut surface with a flat cabinetmaker's file so the two walls butt together tightly. If there are gaps, they can be filled with auto body spot putty. If you are butt-joining walls or roof sections side-by-side, reinforce the seam with a 0.125x0.250-inch strip of Evergreen styrene on the underside of the walls or roof. Test fit all four walls and the roof to be sure they fit tightly before cementing them together.

continued on page 58

The city on Bill Langsdorf's layout (Chapter 13) is a collection of Lionelville buildings that includes 6-14168 Harry's Barber Shop; 6-24182 Lionel Fire House; 6-34124 Anastasia's Bakery; 6-34128 Pharmacy Store; 6-34131 Al's Hardware; 6-24183 Lionelville Esso Gas Station; and 6-12748 Illuminated Station Platform.

All of the major city buildings on Mike Hill's 6x6-foot city layout in this chapter are assembled from Ameri-Towne plastic wall sections. The illuminated marquee is on the Walthers Palace Theater. The Hardware Store is assembled from two Ameri-Towne No. 873 Burke Building kits.

Continued from page 55

»» Painting Structures

Brick building kits are molded in a red plastic, the stone versions in gray plastic. You can, of course, paint the walls other shades of red or beige to match other types of brick. You can also use the dry-brushing technique to apply a slightly lighter or darker color to random bricks to re-create the mottled appearance of real brick walls.

The mortar lines can be accented with a wash of four parts water to one part acrylic paint. The diluted color will settle into the seams to produce the effect of mortar around every brick. Mortar and cement are not really white, but a yellowish gray. A mixture of equal parts Tamiya Desert Yellow acrylic with Tamiya White is close and can be used as-is to paint the sidewalks or concrete foundations. For accenting the mortar lines, dilute the paint with four parts water.

This Fire and Police Station is assembled from one No. 864 Ameri-Towne Fire Station with the front wall on the left and the side walls at the extreme ends. The second fire station front wall is a No. 64 Fire Station Building Front. A No. 868 Police Station is joined on right with a second No. 68 Police Station Building Front. The rear walls are the leftover sidewalls from the 864 Police Station and 864 Fire Station.

Roofs are included with all of the Ameri-Towne kits. You can join them side-by-side with a 0.125x0.250-inch strip of Evergreen styrene to brace the joints. You can use Evergreen 0.060-inch-thick sheet styrene for roofs on the Design Preservation buildings. Since most city roofs are tarred, paint them flat black and simulate the lines and seams with dry-brush sweeps of lighter gray. The Ameri-Towne No. 37 Roof Top Water Tanks are located on most of the roofs. The roof vents are included in some of the Ameri-Towne kits.

»»» Super-Detailing Your City

Ameri-Towne No. 34 Sidewalks are included with most of their kits, and you can buy additional pieces to finish off an entire block. Use flat plywood or particleboard for the streets, but apply a thin layer of spackling plaster to provide some texture. Les Kushner used Luan plywood primed, spackled, sanded, then painted with blackboard paint.

Paint the surface dark gray to simulate tar, or use the concrete gray used for the sidewalks to simulate concrete. Use a paint pen, guided by a ruler, to mark the yellow or white centerlines and parking spaces on the streets. A fine-point black felt tip can be used to mark the expansion joints and cracks in concrete streets or sidewalks.

All of the small details that are part of any city scene are available painted and ready to use. Lionel's 6-24156 Lionelville Street Lamps are similar to the antique-looking Model Power No. 6078 on Mike Hill's layout later in this chapter. Lionel includes a telephone booth in its 6-24197 City Accessory Pack with a pop machine, mailbox, drinking fountain, newspaper vending machine, and trash can. The telephone booth on Mike's layout is from the Life-Like 1851 City Assortment that also includes four fire hydrants, four trash cans, and four fireplugs. Life-Like also offers a

continued on page 64

A few of these Lionelville houses on Mark Cavaliere's layout (Chapter 14) have been painted and modified slightly, and all are weathered with a wash of light gray paint by the crew from Custom Train Layouts. There is a series of Lionelville houses that include (from top left to right) 6-34111 Deluxe Fieldstone House; 6-34109 Large Suburban House I (with an added fence); 6-34108 Suburban House; 6-34110 Estate House; and 6-34109 Large Suburban House I.

The buildings on Mark Cavaliere's layout (Chapter 14) are weathered with a wash of diluted light gray paint to accent the mortar lines and to dull the overall color in one step. This is Lionel's 6-34124 Anastasia's Bakery and 6-34129 Kiddie City Toys with two Lionel 6-24190 Station Platforms and a pair of 6-14098 Mainline Auto Crossing Gates.

The walls of the underground station are Evergreen No. 4504 sheet styrene painted a gloss light yellow to simulate tile.

Continued from page 59
No. 1848 Traffic Light. The illuminated signs are from Light Works by Miller Engineering: Stardust is 65812, Rexall Drugs is 66812, and Patriot Flag Company is 9481.

Most of the figures are from the various Lionelville People Packs, with a few Preiser people in some of the more visible scenes. The automobiles are 1/43-scale die-cast metal from the toy departments of the major chain stores.

Mike Hill's 6x6 City Layout

Mike Hill commissioned the builders at Main Line Hobbies in East Norriton, Pennsylvania, to create his dream layout. Mike wanted a city in his den with a train providing the "living" action. The layout is built on two 3x6-foot tables framed with 1x4-inch wood and cross-braced every 2 feet. The two tables rest on two 3x6 conference tables with folding legs.

The track plan is simple. It's a single main line running around the perimeter of the table. Mike wanted to be able to operate his Lionel 4-6-4 Hudson, which needed a minimum 48-inch curve, so the curves are all 48 inches, leaving room for a 15-inch straight on each of the four sides. Only about a third of the track is visible on the backside of the city, with another 2 feet open in the gallery that represents an underground city terminal— perhaps one track of Grand Central Station.

Les Kushner assembled all of the structures as described earlier in this chapter. The structures all have interior illumination, and the streetlights and signs are also illuminated, as is the underground platform.

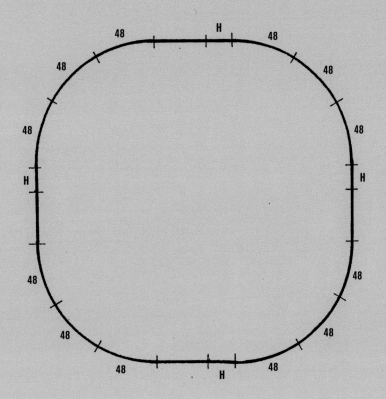

Mark Hill's 6x6 City Layout

Quantity	Symbol	Part No.	Description
4	None	6-12032	10-inch standard straight
12	48	6-12043	48-inch curve (O48)
4	H	6-12024	1/2-straight (5-inch)

Space required is 6x6 feet.

The Corner Liquor Store was assembled from eight kits, made by using just the No. 72 Bill's Place Front Walls to provide the two fronts on the side street.

The Corner Liquor Store is four panels wide and two panels deep, with leftovers from the three kits providing the side and back walls.

The Stardust is assembled from two No. 874 Granato's Grocery kits on the left and a single 878 Ed's Hardware. The Stardust sign is No. 65812 from Light Works by Miller Engineering.

The back walls of this eight-panel-long business block are leftover from the kits that supplied the fronts. The sliding freight door panels are two of the No. 70 Back Wall kits.

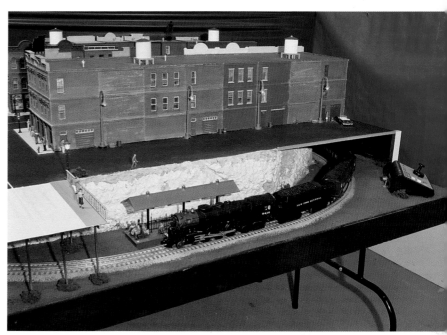

The longest visible section of track is only about 2x6 feet with a Lionel Illuminated Station Platform.

The layout is just 6x6 feet to fit on the top of a pair of 3x6 conference tables. There are seven blocks of city buildings. With the exception of the stand-alone Walthers Theater, all the buildings were assembled from Ameri-Towne Modular Wall System panels. The buildings used in the layout are: stand-alone Walthers Theater; Drug Store (2x1 gray stone panels); Hardware Store (2x1 panels); Stardust Lounge (3x1 panels); and Fire & Police Station (4x1 panels).

The Hotel Building, 6x1s (actually a string of seven all with four walls) left to right is made up of: 873 Burke Building; 875 Lou's Café; 872 Bill's Place; 874 Granato's Grocery; 873 Burke Building; and 878 Ed's Hardware.

The Liquor Store block is a structure comprising massive 2x8 panels and is assembled from two 873 Burke Buildings, two 874 Gramp's Grocery, one 442 Acme Machine, one 872 Bill's Place, one 442 Acme Machine, and one 872 Bill's Place.

The illuminated Patriot Flag Company sign on top of the liquor store block is No. 9481 from Light Works by Miller Engineering.

Here is a Walthers Theater with an illuminated sign. All of the other buildings were assembled from Ameri-Towne Modular Wall System plastic panels.

Most of the figures are from the Lionelville People Packs. The girl in pink is from the Preiser 65313 Truckers w/Hitch Hiker set of four figures.

CHAPTER 7

Portable and Modular FasTrack Model Railroads

We all dream of finding a space for a permanent Lionel model railroad. If, however, you lack the space for even a 5x9-foot layout, consider creating at least one or more portions, or modules, of a larger layout. Combine several of these portable modules, and you and your friends can easily assemble a

model railroad large enough for 30-car trains in an empty garage or, with even larger layouts, in a gymnasium or exhibit hall. Anyone can find space for one of these 2x8 model railroad modules placed, perhaps, on top of a bookcase or on a shelf in the garage above the hood of the car.

There are several modular model railroad clubs that get together every month or so at a train show or conventional center, or in an empty store to assemble a layout as large as 32x48 feet. Your local dealer will know if there are any modular clubs in your area. If not, get together with some friends and create your own. In between these modular model railroad club gatherings, you can operate your own modular segment of that layout, with shorter trains switching industries like the Lionel Log Loader at home.

Portable Lionel Layouts

A Lionel layout assembled on a table tennis table, as shown in *The Lionel FasTrack Book*, is a portable model railroad because it can be folded up into a 2x5-foot platform and stored in a closet. Many Lionel clubs have assembled portable layouts, in addition to a permanent layout, so that they can be displayed and operated at exhibit halls, state fairs, and hobby shows.

An alternative method of assembling a portable Lionel FasTrack layout is to use conference tables with folding legs, as described in Chapter 5. The Chicagoland Lionel Railroad Club (www.clrctrains.com) assembled a

Facing page: Lionel's fantastic replica of the Acela commuter train banks its way around a corner on the Glancy Trains Modular Railroad Club layout.

The Chicagoland Lionel Railroad Club's modular layout is assembled on six 2 1/2x4–foot lightweight tables.

5x12-foot layout on six 2½x4 lightweight tables. The club opted to construct their own 2½x4 tables framed with 1x4-inch boards with a fifth 1x4 down the center and a ¼-inch plywood top. The legs are 1½-inch steel tubes that slide into sockets. The bottom of each leg has a welded-on nut and bolt, so the legs can be adjusted to compensate for uneven floors in exhibit halls.

The track is a simple two-oval with 48-inch curves on the outer oval and 36-inch curves on the inner oval—essentially just an extended version of the double-track plan in Chapter 8. The club changes the locations of the siding and cutoff tracks at every show to present different operating and scenic possibilities.

Modular Layouts

A modular model railroad is one that is built to a specific design on a series of standard tables. The standard design allows any of the tables to be joined to any other table. The tracks on a modular layout are located a specific distance away from the edge of the table, say 3, 9, and 15 inches, to match the 6-inch spacing between Lionel FasTrack curves (36-, 48-, 60-, 72-, and 84-inch diameters). With standard track spacing at each end, any number of modules can be joined to create a variety of combinations.

If you are really short of room, you can assemble a single 2x8-foot module and install enough turnouts in the track, so you can perform switching movements in a small yard or industrial area. If you can convince some of your friends to build similar modules with matching end interfaces, you can assemble all the modules for operations in an empty store or garage.

The Glancy Trains 30x36-foot FasTrack portable modular layout is the work of the Detroit Historical Museum's Glancy Trains Modular Railroad Club (www.glancytrains.

com). The club members are volunteers with the Detroit Historical Museum, which houses a large, permanent Glancy Trains layout. The modular layout is assembled at train shows throughout the region to promote the museum, but enough modules exist to expand the layout into more than four times this size when space permits, in an exhibit hall for example.

Mark Farver and the Glancy Trains Modular Railroad Club crew created their own modular design with very clever straight and outside 90-degree turn modules. The basic "A" module is a 2½x8-foot with three parallel straight tracks. Within the module, switches can be installed with sidings or crossovers from any of the three tracks to the others. Module "B" is a 3x3 outside corner with each corner cut at a 45-degree angle to leave 2-foot-wide ends and a 6-inch notch in the inner corner.

They have also created a multi-module

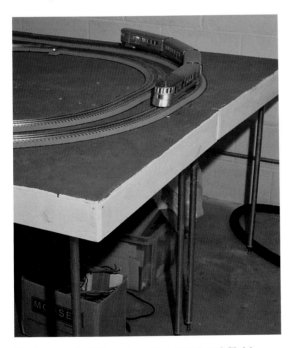

The legs on the Chicagoland Lionel Railroad Club's modules are 1 1/2–inch steel tubes with adjusting bolts and nuts welded to the bottom of each leg, and the legs are bolted to the inside edges of the table.

set to allow an inside corner to be linked to two of the outside corners. Two or more of the standard A modules can be joined into another multi-module set that can include a two- or three-module-long multi-track yard, with only the extreme ends of the module's three tracks spaced to match other A or B modules. They use alligator-clip-style heavy-duty spring clamps to hold modules together with multi-wire plugs for the track wiring, and each module also has its own transformer to power any accessories placed on it.

The club's modules are screwed together from grade A 1x4-inch lumber with a ½-inch Luan plywood tabletop. The track is screwed directly into the tabletop, and although it is loud, the noise level seems just right in the vast exhibit halls where the layout is usually assembled.

The table legs are folding-steel tubular types from conference tables with steel caps threaded for ¼-inch bolts so the legs can be adjusted to keep the layout level on uneven exhibit hall floors. The tabletop is 34 inches from the floor.

The layout operates with the Lionel TrainMaster Command Control, which allows three or four trains to run on each of three tracks as long as all the trains are traveling in the same direction. The massive size of many of the layouts the club assembles provides enough running room so three trains can often be spaced 30 feet or more apart.

I modified the Glancy Trains Modular Club's design slightly for the 14x22-foot layout in the plan. The nearest track is 3 inches from the table edge, and the other two tracks are at 9 and 15 inches from the table edge. The tracks at both ends of the module are recessed 2½ inches so a 5-inch half straight can be inserted as the modules are assembled. The straight track on the 8-foot sections is custom cut, with 2½ inches

continued on page 78

The Detroit Historical Museum's Glancy Trains Modular Club assembled this layout for the 2007 National Model Railroad Association's annual convention in Detroit. The module to the lower left is an Outside Curve Module (A); the 2 1/2x8-foot Straight Modules (B) join it in the lower right and upper left.

14x22 Modular Layout

This layout can be assembled from just three basic modules: Module A is 2 1/2x8 feet with three parallel tracks; Module B is 3x3 feet overall with two corners cut off at the 2-foot mark; Multi-Module Set C is an Inside Curve and is used primarily to create ess curves.

Quantity	Symbol	Part No.	Description	Quantity	Symbol	Part No.	Description
106*	None	6-12032	10-inch standard straight	12	36	6-12015	36-inch curve (036)
43	H	6-12024	1/2 straight	18	48	6-12046	48-inch curve (048)
1	N	6-12025	4 1/2-inch straight	24	60	6-12056	60-inch curve (060)
7	S	6-12073	1 3/8-inch insulated straight	24	72	6-12041	72-inch curve (072)
12	X	6-12032	6-inch custom-cut 10-inch "standard" straight				

This assembly of modules is 14x22 feet, but it can range from 6x14 to 180x276 or larger.

*Note: With the long straights on this layout you can substitute six of the 30-inch-long 6-12042 straights for each run of three of the standard 10-inch 6-12032 straights.

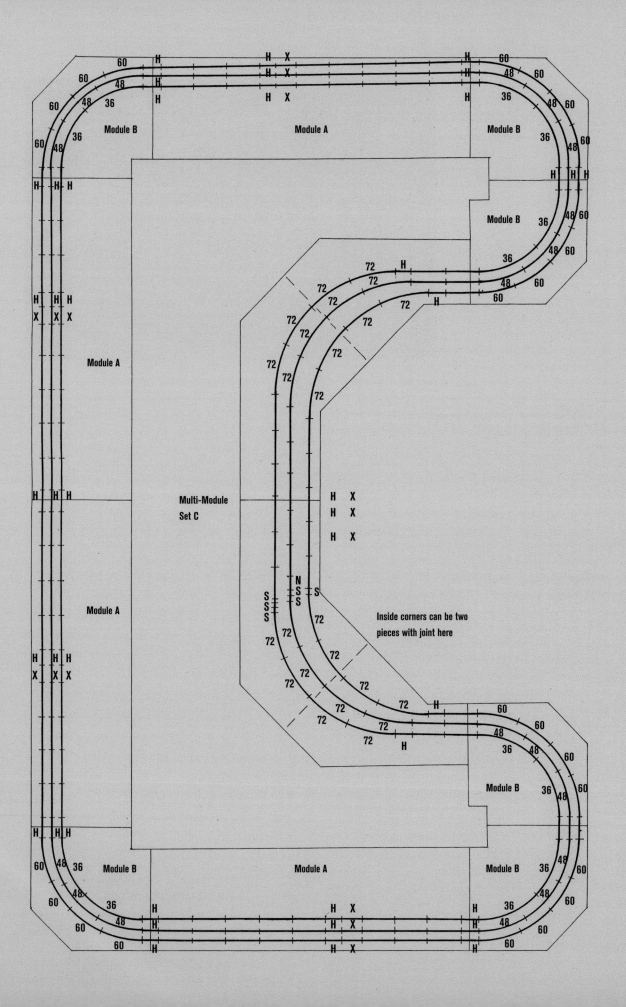

The straight modules (Module A) are 2 1/2x8 feet, but there are some special multi-module sets of two or three 8-foot modules that incorporate six-track freight and passenger yards, and industrial districts. This six-track yard is on three 3x8-foot modules. In the distance is a 4x8-foot roundhouse and locomotive service center module.

Continued from page 75

removed from each end to provide for 5-inch joining straights. The remaining straight is 91 inches long. Lionel only offers 10-inch and 5-inch straights which alone cannot be combined to create 91 inches of track. I have used a 5-inch (half straights) across each module joint for these modules. This leaves an odd length on the 8-foot modules, because 96 inches less 5 inches is 91 inches. I suggest using a combination of a 5-inch piece and a 10-inch piece, and cutting with a razor saw 4 inches from the center of the 10-inch piece. Next, rejoin the ends with plastic cement to produce a 6-inch piece. Clip wires beneath the ballast to provide electrical current across the cut. Assemble the 6-inch, the 5-inch, and eight of the 10-inch pieces, and you will have the 91 inches needed. The 10-inch track that is shortened to 6 inches is marked "X" on the plan.

There is a far simpler, third alternative: Make the 8-foot table length just an inch shorter at 95 inches and forget about cutting any of the track sections. If all of your straight modules are 30x95 they will be just as versatile as the inch-longer modules, and most of us find it easier to cut wood than to cut and splice track.

The two "C" modules are really a joined set, or a multi-module set. Note that this multi-module set C and the two-curve modules "B" form a double ess curve that is 16 feet long (including the necessary two B curves, one at each end), so it can be inserted in place of any two standard 2x8-foot "A" modules.

There was enough room to include the broad 72-inch curves on all three tracks. The straights are a rather random length to allow all of the curves to be a constant 72 inches. Lionel's short filler pieces fill the gaps. The three tracks are 64⅛, 57¼, and 51⅜ inches long. The 64⅛-inch outer track can be fitted with three 1⅜-inch straights plus six 10-inch straights; the 57¼-inch middle track with two 1⅜-inch straights plus a 4½-inch plus five standard 10-inch straights; and the inner track with one 1⅜-inch straight and five 10-inch straights. This set is designed so that the interface ends are 10-inch straights with the extreme ends of tracks extending past the end of the module 2½ inches to be joined to any A or B module. The joint between the two halves of this multi-module set are covered by 10-inch straights, which are

The wide-angle camera lens has distorted this ess curve. Note that the Inside Curve Module B (lower left) has the tracks near the outer edge while the Outside Curve Multi-Module Set C (upper left) has the tracks near the inside edge of the module. Most of the buildings here are older K-Line, including the 41506 Ranch and 40731 Texaco Gas Station.

removed when the module is disassembled. The module halves are 5½x6½ feet, which can be awkward to handle. It is wise to build them in two halves, split along the dotted line and clamped together like all the other modules.

If you make the standard straight modules 95 inches long, this inside curve multi-module set has to be 2 inches shorter. The 190-inch-long version has three straights: 62⅛, 55¼, and 49⅜ inches long. You can span that 62⅛-inch distance with three 1⅜-inch, four 4½-inch, and four 10-inch straights; the 55¼ with three 1¾-inch and five 10-inch sections; and the 49⅜ with one 1⅜-inch section, four 4½-inch sections, and three 10-inch sections.

Just because these modules were designed for a club doesn't mean you can't use them for your home layout. The modular construction means that the railroad will always be portable, and you can expand or contract it to fit whatever space you have available. If you choose, just make four of the 3x3 corner modules and two straight modules to assemble a 6x14 triple-track oval. If you find more space, you can expand that oval with another pair of 2½x8 modules to expand to 6x22. Build the multi-module inside curve set and assemble a layout like that in the plan.

CHAPTER 8

Main-Line Two-Train 5x9 Layout

The most exciting scene on even the largest and most complex Lionel layouts is that of two opposing trains thundering toward one another, magically passing without the slightest reduction in speed to head off in their opposite directions. Sure, it's great to watch a single train thundering around as each car snaps

out of the curve and onto the straight. Watching two trains provides more than double the thrill, however, because you add the sight of the two trains seemingly headed for the ultimate derailment. You can re-create that action on a layout as small as 5x9 feet, just like this one.

The Double-Track Main Line

Most of the layouts in this book have been designed and built to re-create a double-track main line, though Les Kushner's layout in Chapter 12 has three double-track main lines. When you look at the track plans for some of the more complex layouts in the later chapters, it may be hard to believe that they are nothing but convoluted double-track ovals. Every one of these layouts was built and designed by very experienced modelers, many of them designed and built by professionals. If that combined wisdom suggests that a double-track main line may bring your dreams of a tabletop model railroad to reality, perhaps you should consider a similar design for your own Lionel FasTrack layout.

»» The Lionel FasTrack Double-Track System

FasTrack is designed to allow the trains to operate side-by-side without the overhang from the inner train sideswiping the outer train. For the longest cars and locomotives on the smallest curves, the tracks must be separated about 6 inches through the curves. FasTrack is offered in 36-, 48-, 60-, 72-,

Facing page: Two trains operate independently on this table tennis table–size layout.

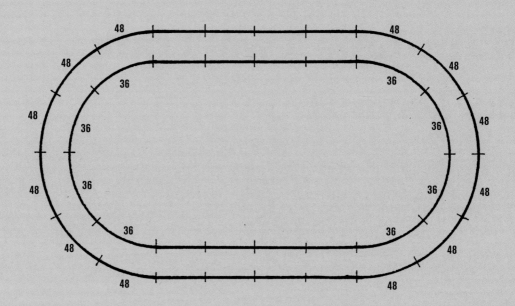

Les Kushner's Two-Train 5x9 Layout

Quantity	Symbol	Part No.	Description
16	None	6-12032	10-inch standard straight
8	36	6-12015	36-inch curve (O36)
12	48	6-12046	48-inch curve (O48)

Space required is 5x9 feet.

A Polar Express train operating on the 48-inch outer oval, with a 6-38605 PRR 0-4-0 steam locomotive pulling a short freight on the 36-inch oval.

and 84-inch-diameter curves to provide that 6-inch spacing. Matching 36-, 60-, and 72-inch switches are also available. When the tracks are straight, they can be moved closer together, as close as 4 inches apart. There are examples of these closer-spaced parallel straight tracks in the freight yard in the lower left of Mark Cavaliere's layout in Chapter 14 and on the two long double-track main lines on Vito Glimco's layout in Chapter 16.

»»» The Convoluted Double-Track Oval

The concept of the double-track oval can be expanded, and the design twisted and contorted to suit a larger space. Les Kushner's 12x12-foot layout in Chapter 12 includes three complete double-track ovals separated on three levels. At a glance, they might not look like double-track ovals, but study the plans carefully, tracing the routes of the trains with your fingertip, and you will see that even the lower-level layout is just a much-convoluted double-track oval.

Train operation becomes a bit more complex if you want the trains to be able to move from the inner outer oval or if you want to be able to reverse the trains from either direction. Again, the lower-level plan in Chapter 12 provides both crossovers from the inner oval outer oval and reverse-loop cutoff tracks. There's more information on wiring the tracks for two-train operation and on reverse loops in *The Lionel FasTrack Book*.

»»» Two Trains on a Table Tennis Top

Les Kushner of Main Line Hobbies in East Norriton, Pennsylvania, built the double-track

Each train has its own independent power supply, with the two CW-80 Power Supply units on the right.

main-line layout in this chapter. Les wanted to demonstrate just how exciting Lionel can be in a space as small as a 5x9-foot table tennis table. For him, there was only one design choice: a double-track main line. His customers could see the action that made the operation of two trains much, much more than twice as exciting as just operating a single train.

Les has added scenery to this layout with the idea in mind that watching a train (or even two trains) sweep around and around a bare oval gives little suggestion of how quickly the train is traveling. To provide the measure of the trains' speeds, there must be some non-moving objects for the trains to pass, be they signals, crossings, stations, action industries, trees, bridges, hills, or valleys. This compact layout has most of those static elements for the trains to pass. No doubt, scenery makes the sight of two trains plummeting toward one another even more exciting to watch.

This double-track oval was built to demonstrate scenery techniques and to show just how well a Lionel layout can be assembled in a space as small as a 5x9 table tennis tabletop. The track is placed directly

on 2-inch-thick sheets of pink Dow Corning extruded Styrofoam. The sheets are glued together edge to edge. An oval with 48-inch curves was laid around the perimeter of the tabletop, and an oval with 36-inch curves fits neatly inside. Two transformers are used, one for each of the ovals.

The mountains are carved from stacks of 2-inch pink Styrofoam as described in Chapter 5. The 2-inch foam was cut away on one side of the layout to leave only about ½ inch to create a valley to be crossed by a truss bridge. When the final scenery was shaped, the locations of the track edges were marked with a felt-tip pen, and the track was removed. The Styrofoam hills and valley were then covered with a hard plaster coat topped with brown latex paint. The areas to be covered with grass were coated with artist's matte medium then sprinkled with Scenic Express ground-foam grass and real dirt, sifted through a flour strainer, for the roads. When the scenery was complete, the track was replaced, held in place with a few dabs of silicone bathtub caulk. The FasTrack itself is already scenic, with simulated ballast and ties, so with the track in place, the railroad is ready to run!

The trees on this 5x9-foot layout are Life-Like products.

The mountains are carved from stacks of 2-inch-thick pink Styrofoam then coated with plaster and painted with latex interior wall paint.

CHAPTER 9

Doug Waller's 6x12 Layout

This model railroad was custom-built by Doug Waller for one of the customers at the Train Station in Mountain Lakes, New Jersey, and is designed to provide virtually every kind of operation possible. It is a complex layout with a clever combination of switches, and it would be difficult to squeeze any more track into a 6x12-foot layout. When you learn about

the different possibilities of routing trains around a layout like this, you see that each track has a specific purpose. There are examples of some of these track arrangements on nearly every other layout in this book, each allowing expanded versions of the operations that are possible on this 6x12 layout.

This layout is built on two separate 6x6 tables assembled from a frame of 1x4s with 2x4 legs and ½-inch plywood for the tabletops. A layer of 2-inch-thick pink extruded Styrofoam covers the tabletops. Sheets of green simulated felt intended to line jewelry boxes are used to simulate grass across the full width and length of the tabletop. The tables are bolted together so they can be separated for easier transportation when the layout is moved.

Passenger Operations

The excitement of Lionel, for many fans, is the choice of accessories that are available. Most of those accessories need enough track to provide the run-by action that makes the accessories so useful and exciting. On Doug's layout, for example, there's a long double-ended siding on the outer oval. The tracks are spaced just far enough apart so the magnificent Lionel No. 115 Station can fit between them. The two tracks then become a passenger terminal, not just two parallel tracks.

Ideally, you can operate two complete passenger trains, one westbound and the other eastbound. Park the eastbound train on the outer siding at the passenger terminal while the westbound does a few dozen laps as it heads for the next town, 377 miles away. When that journey is complete,

Facing page: Six of Lionel's station platforms with the No. 115 Passenger Station rest between the two parallel tracks on the outer oval.

Doug Waller's 6x12-foot layout is chock-full of FasTrack, with an inner and outer oval, overlapped reverse loops (to form a figure eight), a passing siding to hold a third train, and six stub-ended industrial sidings.

imagine the station to be that westbound train's destination and park it. Repeat the process with the second eastbound train, running in the opposite direction. Each of the trains needs time for passengers to disembark, so the sight of one train running while the other is resting is realistic.

Moving Trains from Point to Point

One of the classic operating patterns that model railroaders re-create is that of running a train from one terminal to another. That's what happens on a real railroad when, say, a train originates in Los Angeles and reaches a final destination in Chicago. The train has operated from point to point, from Los Angeles to Chicago. On Doug's layout, each of the three-track yards is tucked into a reverse loop. You can consider the right reverse loop (the one that includes the diagonal track that runs from the upper-right to lower-left) to be a self-contained town. When trains reach this town, they can be rearranged on the three stub-ended tracks and reversed to head out to the opposite town. Consider the left-hand reverse loop (with the diagonal track that heads upper-left to lower-right) to be a second town. On this layout, you can consider the outer oval and its station to be a third town, perhaps midway between the first and second towns. To include that station in the trains' path from point to point you would, however, need to connect the outer oval and the inner oval with two pairs of crossovers.

Loop-to-Loop Operations

Most of the layouts in the later chapters have at least one cutoff track that creates a reverse loop. The reverse loop is what it sounds like, a loop shaped like a falling drop of rain with a switch at the upper or point end. The reverse loop is the portion of a layout's track where

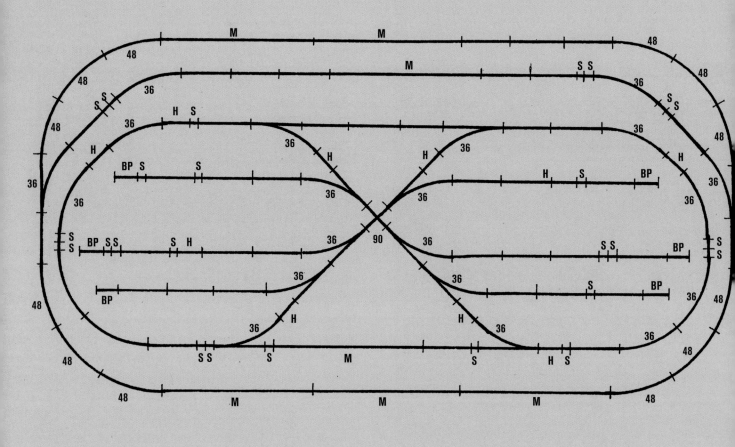

Doug Waller's 6x12 Layout

Quantity	Symbol	Part No.	Description
38	None	6-12032	10-inch standard straight
7	M	6-12042	30-inch straight
6	BP	6-12035	Lighted Bumper or
	BP	6-12059	Earthen Bumper
6	H	6-12024	1/2-straight (5-inch)

Quantity	Symbol	Part No.	Description
24	S	6-12073	1 3/8-inch insulated straight
10	36	6-12015	36-inch curve (O36)
6	36	6-12045	36-inch switch left (O36)
6	36	6-12046	36-inch switch right (O36)
12	48	6-12043	48-inch curve (O48)

Space required is 6x12 feet.

a train can be rerouted, so it exits the area running in the opposite direction it entered.

This compact layout actually has two reverse loops placed on top of one another, with diagonal cutoff tracks meeting at the 90-degree crossing in the middle of the layout. You can designate the right-hand reverse loop (and the three-track yard inside it) to be, say, Los Angeles, and the left-hand reverse loop (also with its three stub-ended sidings) to be Chicago.

For demonstration purposes, imagine a three-car train pulling out of any of the three right stub-end sidings (we'll call that loop and three tracks Chicago) and heading out to run around and around on the inside oval. Run the train for as many laps as you think it might take to reach Chicago

from Los Angeles and throw the switches so the train can enter the diagonal track to reach the left reverse loop at Los Angeles.

Run the train across the diagonal track and back out onto the oval, and it is heading back toward Chicago. You can repeat the process again and again. With the three stub-ended sidings in each town, you also have the option of rearranging the train when it reaches Chicago and again when it reaches Los Angeles, as described later in this chapter.

The two overlapping reversing loops are located on the inner oval in this example, and there is no connection between the inner and outer ovals. Assembling the track so there is no track connection between the two ovals makes it easier to wire the layout for two trains, because all you need are two

The Lionel Oil Derrick and the blue and red Lionel Log Loader are on the opposite end of this 6x12-foot layout.

Two of Lionel's No. 315 Post War Truss Bridges (repainted gray) beside the K-Line Diner.

transformers, each with a single pair of wires connected to the 6-12016 Terminal Track Section on the designated oval, as described in Chapter 2. If you install two pairs of right- and two pairs of left-hand switches like those on the left of the lower level on Gary Rupert's layout in Chapter 11, the trains from the outer oval can be routed to the inner oval to use those reversing loops. You'll need one pair of switches to get the trains onto the inner oval and the second pair to get the trains back onto the outer oval. With that modification, you can operate just one passenger train, because it can be both "eastbound" and "westbound." Start it at the station on the outer oval and, after a few laps, switch the train into the inner oval and across the diagonal track so it can exit the inner oval to enter the station on the outer oval in the opposite direction. Run it around in the opposite direction for a few laps, then route the train back into the inner oval and through a reverse loop so it can reappear at the station from the opposite direction as if it had made the journey to Chicago and is now headed back to Los Angeles.

There is more information on reverse loops and some simple loop-to-loop track plans in *The Lionel FasTrack Book*.

Where to Install Uncoupling and Operating Tracks

None of the plans in this book indicate where to install uncoupling or operating tracks because they are only needed for specific types of operations. Any of the sidings can be used to store a train as long as the train is shorter than the length of the siding, so the train does not foul the main line. If you want to use any of the sidings to rearrange trains or just to provide a place to spot a car at an action industry like Log Loader, you will need to install a 6-12020 Uncoupling Track on the siding side of the switch, so you can uncouple the train from the car. If you want to rearrange the cars in the train (or if the car you want to spot is in the middle of the train), you will need a second Uncoupling Track on the adjacent track (even if that track is the main line). You will also need a 6-12054 Operating Track to activate any dump or unloading cars beside Log Loader or Coal Elevator.

Operations at Industries

There are two three-track freight yards on the inner oval on this plan. The tracks are spaced far enough apart so action accessories like the Lionel Log Loader or Coal Elevator will drop right in. It's wise to buy two operating cars to match the action industry. If you are purchasing the Log Loader, for example, buy two automatic log-dumping cars, so one car can be spotted on the unloading side of the Log Loader to dump its loads and the second car from some distant place can be moved into the unloading side of the Log Loader to accept a load of logs. Run the empty car around the layout for a few dozen laps to simulate its journey back to the woods, then return it to the unloading side of the Log Loader. Similarly, take that first loaded log car for a few dozen laps around the layout to simulate its journey to a distant lumberyard. After a while, spot the loaded car on the unloading side of the Log Loader and repeat this entire sequence. As you can imagine, it's far more credible to re-create the logging and lumber industry with two cars rather than watching the same single car. You can, of course, re-create the operation of a coal dealer with the Lionel Coal Elevator. You can also create other industries with barrels, blocks of ice, or packages using other Lionel action accessories.

Operations in Freight Yards

The three yard tracks can also be used like those in a real railroad yard to rearrange trains' cars. To simulate real railroad yard operations, consider one of the three tracks being for eastbound cars and the second track for westbound cars. The third track can be used as a make-up track, where you collect the cars to make a new train. Assume, for an operating session, that a four-car freight arrives from the south with two cars for the east and two cars for the west. The locomotive would back the train to uncouple the two west cars on the diagonal track, and then pull forward and back into the first track to deposit, or spot, the two east cars. It would repeat the process to deposit the west cars on a second track. Later, a second train might arrive with four more cars to be divided with two more cars on the east and two more on the west track, leaving you with a four-car west train that can be picked up by a locomotive and headed out around the layout to the west. The accumulated four cars for the east can be picked up by a second locomotive and headed out in the opposite direction around the layout, toward the east.

Doug Waller's 6x12 Operating Action Layout

This track plan was created by Doug Waller to provide as much operation as possible in the space. Essentially, there is just a 36-inch inner oval and a 48-inch outer oval. The two ovals are not connected by any crossovers, so a separate transformer can be used to control each oval. The inner oval is a complex arrangement of switches and a 90-degree crossing to allow trains traveling in either direction to be reversed. There are also six industrial sidings spaced to allow operation of the Lionel Log Loader and the Coal Elevator. The outer oval has a passing siding that can be used to store a third train.

The layout includes the Lionel No. 115 Station, new Station Platforms, Gantry Crane, Oil Drum Loader, Yard Tower, Log Loader, two stamped-metal No. 315 Post War Truss Bridges, Water Tower with real water, K-Line Diner, and the American Flyer Coal Station. There's room for even more Lionel action accessories if the owner decides to expand his empire.

CHAPTER 10

Michael Fritschie's 8x12 Layout

Michael Fritschie had room in the attic of his home for an 8x12-foot Lionel layout. Michael's passion is modern freight trains, so he designed the layout to re-create the action of today's freights. The four diagonal tracks in the center of the layout are a reduced re-creation of the real railroads' freight yards. Several industrial sidings around the layout serve specific industries just as they do on the real railroads.

He designed the layout by laying the track on the floor, then building tables to provide enough space for about 3 inches of clearance on all sides and table edges. The tables are assembled from 1x4-inch boards on edge with 2x4 legs, a ½-inch plywood top, and a layer of 2-inch pink extruded Styrofoam.

The track plan is an interesting variation on the double-track oval. The outer oval is bent into an L shape. The inner oval is actually a figure eight (follow the train's path along the two diagonal tracks) with a 90-degree crossing and a bypass track to a simple oval. Two crossovers connect the outer oval to the inner figure eight. There are seven stub-ended sidings that can be used for rearranging trains, for action industries, or to store short trains.

Reversing Operations at a Wye

A wye track arrangement in the lower-right of the plan allows trains to be reversed. The wye is actually a triangle with a switch at each of the three corners. Trace the path of a train entering the wye from any of the three corners. When the train is clear of the switch where it entered the first leg of the wye, throw the switch and

Facing page: Michael Fritschie used the Lionel animated No. 6-14211 Road Crew to provide more action near the carnival in the city scene.

back the train through the second leg of wye. When the train clears that second switch, throw that switch and pull the train forward along the third leg of the wye. The train will exit the wye through that first switch, heading the opposite direction it entered. The wye is used on virtually every real railroad in every town or city where operations might require that the entire train, the locomotive, or just one or two cars be reversed. The wye is particularly common in larger passenger terminals where trains must back into the passenger shed. The reverse loops described in Chapter 9 are actually on real railroads.

Hauling Freight in 8x12 Feet

Michael Fritschie's layout is operated with the Lionel Legacy Control System, so three or four trains can be in action at once. Michael has included signals that are activated from green to red by the Lionel No. 6-14111 Infrared Motion Detector.

The left side of the layout is covered with a 6-inch-high platform cut from ½-inch plywood to support a small city scene complete with a park and carnival. Michael elected to screw the track to the tabletop before adding the scenery.

He masked the ties, rails, and most of the ballast but allowed the green foam and dirt texturing to spill slightly onto the edges of the ballast to create an even more realistic FasTrack. If he elects to move the track for additional sidings or to rearrange some of the curves, the scenery texturing can be reapplied in those areas.

The left half of Michael Fritschie's layout is detailed with a city elevated 6 inches above the tracks.

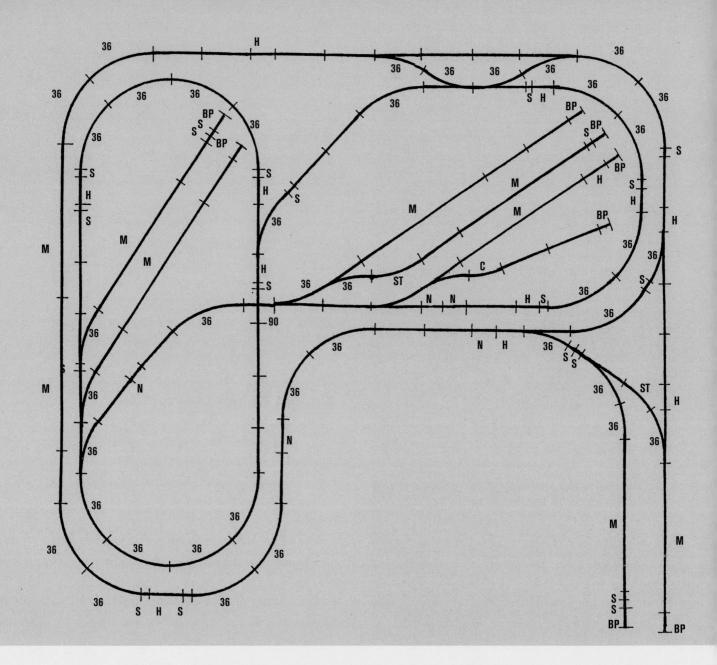

Michael Fritschie's 8x12 Layout

Quantity	Symbol	Part No.	Description
27*	None	6-12032	10-inch standard straight
6	M	6-12042	30-inch straight
8	BP	6-12059	Earthen Bumper or
		6-12035	Lighted Bumper
13	H	6-12024	1/2 straight
4	N	6-12025	4 1/2-inch straight
20	S	6-12073	1 3/8-inch insulated straight

Quantity	Symbol	Part No.	Description
1	C	6-12023	1/4 of 36-inch curve (O36)
3	ST	6-12022	1/2 of 36-inch curve (O36)
5	36	6-12045	36-inch switch left (O36)
11	36	6-12046	36-inch switch right (O36)
25	36	6-12015	36-inch curve (O36)
1	90	6-12019	90-degree crossover

Space required is 8x12 feet.

*Note: The 36-inch switch pairs at crossings and on stub-ended sidings have the 1/2 of a 36-inch curve (6-12022) removed.

A four-track yard occupies the left half of the layout.

On the right edge of the layout, a Norfolk Southern Tank Train is rolling through one leg of the wye. The tower on the right is Lionel 6-14227 Yard Tower, and the Lionel 6-34145 Scrap Yard is on the left.

The stub end of the wye track and a stub-ended siding occupy a foot-wide shelf on the right corner of the layout, with the Lionel Barrel Loader on the siding.

The four-arch brick viaduct is a Mountains in Minutes No. 827 Viaduct HO scale bridge, but it is compatible with Lionel.

A modified Lionel No. 395 Floodlight Tower and two No. 65 Yard Lights provide illumination for the industrial area. The crane is a die-cast metal model from Norscot.

CHAPTER 11

Gary Rupert's 8x14 Layout

Lionel railroaders have at least one thing in common—we like to run trains. For some of us, it's great fun to push a single car in or out of a siding. For all of us, however, there's a special thrill just watching a long freight respond to our commands at the throttle and sitting back as the train magically picks its way through a maze of switches and curves, and, perhaps, through tunnels and over bridges. Doug Waller designed this 8x14-foot layout to provide such train-running action for its owner, Gary Rupert, and his young son.

Operations in 8x14 Feet

Doug Waller's track plan is, again, two convoluted ovals, but these are bent into a U shape, with a third bent-oval on the upper level. Crossovers connect the lower-level inner and outer ovals, and a track ramped from the lower upper level with the Lionel Graduated Trestle Set connects the upper-level and lower-level tracks. There are two reversing loop cutoffs on the lower level, so trains traveling in either direction can be reversed. A single cutoff on the upper level allows trains to be reversed so they can head back down to the lower level.

At the moment, Gary is running a three-unit Santa Fe F3ABA set of diesels at the head of a four-car train of extruded aluminum replicas of the Santa Fe's "Super Chief" cars. Usually, this train stays on one outer oval and its mostly 48-inch curves. The two freight trains have shorter locomotives and much shorter cars, so they look best on the tighter 36-inch curves that are more common on this layout. The two freight trains have the option

Facing page: The Lionel replica of New York Central's Alco RS-3 is on the upper level, with a Santa Fe F3ABA set of diesels emerging from the tunnel portal onto the lower level.

The scenery on the right end of the lower level is complete, but the embankments around the upper level are not yet installed.

of negotiating either the inner oval on the lower level or traversing the upper level. The Lionel TrainMaster Command Control allows completely independent control of each of the three trains (and 96 more, should he choose).

Scenery Is an Option

Scenery can be an option on any model railroad. The layout in this chapter and Doug Waller's in Chapter 15 are completed to the track and wiring stage, while Mark Cavaliere's

in Chapter 14 is ready for final wiring and some final scenery touch up. These layouts will, ultimately, be completely scened, but they can provide the kind of inspiration and information you need to build a layout of your own just as they are. On Gary Rupert's layout, for example, you can see how the upper-level track is mounted on 1x6- and 1x4-inch boards, as well as how the finished scenery will be developed.

There are two 4x8-foot and one 3x4 layout tables, bolted together so they can be disassembled if Gary ever needs to move the layout. The typical 1x4-inch framework with ½-inch plywood tabletop is used, but in this case the tabletop is recessed about an inch below the level of the 1x6 outer frames—1x4s support the plywood as cross braces. The legs are 4x4s. The scenery on the flat areas of the lower level is simply simulated ballast and coal spread around the tracks, held in place with a thorough soaking in artist's matte medium mixed with equal parts water. The mountains and the embankments that will be installed beside the upper-level tracks are plaster-impregnated gauze or plaster cloth draped over wadded newspapers. When set, the plaster is painted with latex interior wall paint.

The right end of the layout has a mountain complete with tunnels for both lower- and upper-level tracks.

The tunnel portals are pre-painted foam moldings from Scenic Express.

The layout is operated with the Lionel TrainMaster Command Control system, so Gary Rupert and his son can control three or more trains at once. The 18 switches are all operated by these FasTrack Remote Control levers.

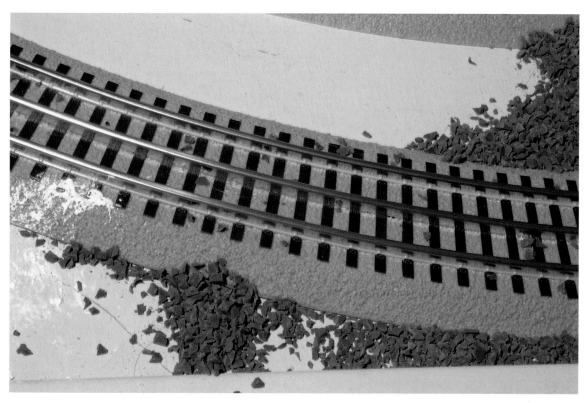

The loose ballast on the lower level will be held in place with a 50-50 mixture of artist's matte medium and water.

The Lionel 6-14211 Road Crew operates with the men moving as if they were building a road. It is blended into the scenery on the lower level of the layout with a mixture of dark and light gray simulated ballast.

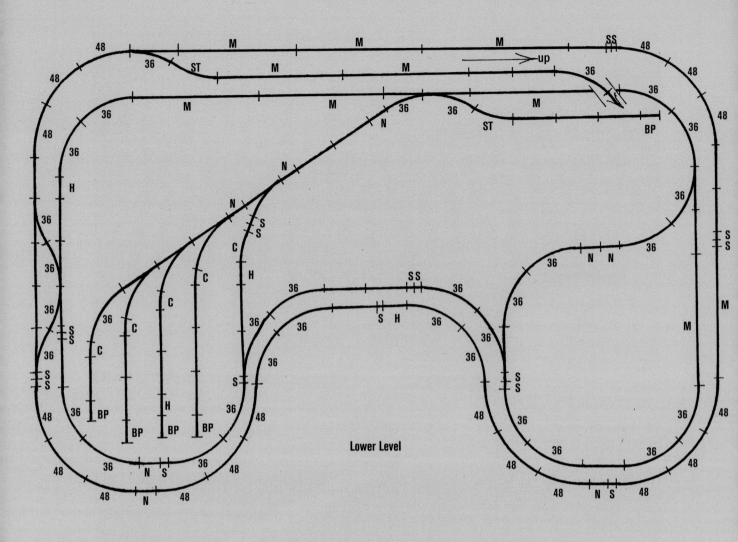

Lower Level

Gary Rupert's 8x14 Layout

Quantity	Symbol	Part No.	Description	Quantity	Symbol	Part No.	Description
32	None	6-12032	10-inch "standard" straight	2	ST	6-12022	1/2 of 36-inch curve (036)
14	M	6-12042	30-inch straight	5	C	6-12023	1/4 of 36-inch curve (036)
5	BP	6-12059	Earthen bumper or	35	36	6-12015	36-inch curve (036)
		6-12035	Lighted bumper	10	36	6-12045	36-inch switch left (036)
10	H	6-12024	1/2-straight	7	36	6-12046	36-inch switch right (036)
6	N	6-12025	4 1/2-inch straight	18	48	6-12043	48-inch curve (048)
19	S	6-12073	1 3/8-inch insulated straight				

Space required is 8x14 feet. The 36-inch switch pairs at crossings and on stub-ended sidings have the 1/2 of a 36-inch curve (6-12022) removed. The upper level connects to the lower level at "A" on the two plans.

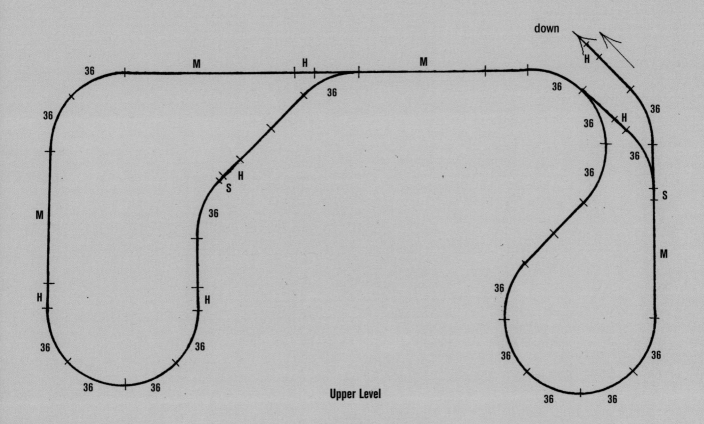

down

Upper Level

CHAPTER 12

Les Kushner's 12x12 Three-Level Layout

Les Kushner wanted to create the most dramatic layout possible in just a 12x12-foot area. When you watch the result of his effort in full operation, you have no doubt he succeeded.

Lionel trains are not designed to be quiet. Part of the thrill of watching just one Lionel train operate is that you can hear and feel that it is a truly hefty assortment of cars with a massive locomotive. Lionel trains don't just roll down the tracks, they thunder their way around the layout.

With Les' layout, the sound and action are multiplied by six. This layout allows six trains to operate at once, even with conventional power supplies, because there are six completely independent routes. On this layout, though, the sound has a third dimension because the six thundering trains are arrayed vertically with almost a foot between each pair. This third dimension gives the effect of surround sound.

Three Railroads in One Space

The layout is actually three layouts stacked on top of one another. There is no upgrade or downgrade to connect any level with any other. I have, therefore, treated the layout as three separate plans because they are not, in fact, connected by any track—only by geography. The layout was designed for running, not switching one car at a time, so there are no stub-ended sidings on any of the levels.

Facing page: A K-Line New Haven Electric Locomotive and the Polar Express pass on the middle level. The station is the No. 133 Lighted Passenger Station with a 6-12961 Lionel News Stand with Horn and No. 38 Water Tower.

Operations on Three Levels

That thrill of watching two trains traveling in opposite directions is repeated three times on this layout. The upper and middle levels are designed for just running trains. The lower level, however, includes several alternate routes. The lower level is a complex design of two reverse loop cutoffs so trains can be reversed from either direction, but essentially it is just two contorted ovals with a passing siding on each oval to hold a third and fourth train. The middle level has no switches at all—just a place to run two trains continuously. Similarly, the third level is designed to run two trains, with the inner loop compressed in the center to form a loop-to-loop line for just one train. The layout allows six trains to be in operation at once, with storage sidings for two more.

Building a Three-Level Layout

The layout is built on substantial tables assembled with 1x4-inch vertical boards with 2x4 legs. The 12x12-foot area is divided into five separate tables, each with its own set of legs. The tables' edges are joined to the adjacent table with carriage bolts, washers, and nuts. The layout can thus be disassembled to be moved. The layout was actually built by Les Kushner for one of the customers of Main Line Hobbies in Norriton, Pennsylvania, so it was moved from the store to the customer's home.

The track is laid on three levels, the lowest of which is supported by a layer of 2-inch pink extruded Styrofoam. The second level is supported by four more layers of 2-inch Styrofoam cut to expose the tracks on the lowest level. The third level is supported by three layers of the 2-inch Styrofoam with a 2-inch layer on top. There is no track

Les Kushner's 12x12-foot layout is actually three layouts, each separated by about 8 vertical inches.

connection from the upper level to the second or lowest levels. The layers of Styrofoam were cut to match joints in the five tables.

The scenery was carved directly into pink Styrofoam then covered with a rough layer of dark gray-colored plaster, as shown in Chapter 5. The vertical walls along the back of the layout are covered with ¼-inch plywood with oval access holes for the hidden tracks on the lower and middle levels.

Left: Four of the Lionel Carnival Action accessories fit inside one of the loops on the upper level.

The sides and rear of the layout are covered with sheets of 1/4-inch plywood. The holes are for access-hidden tracks on the lower and middle levels.

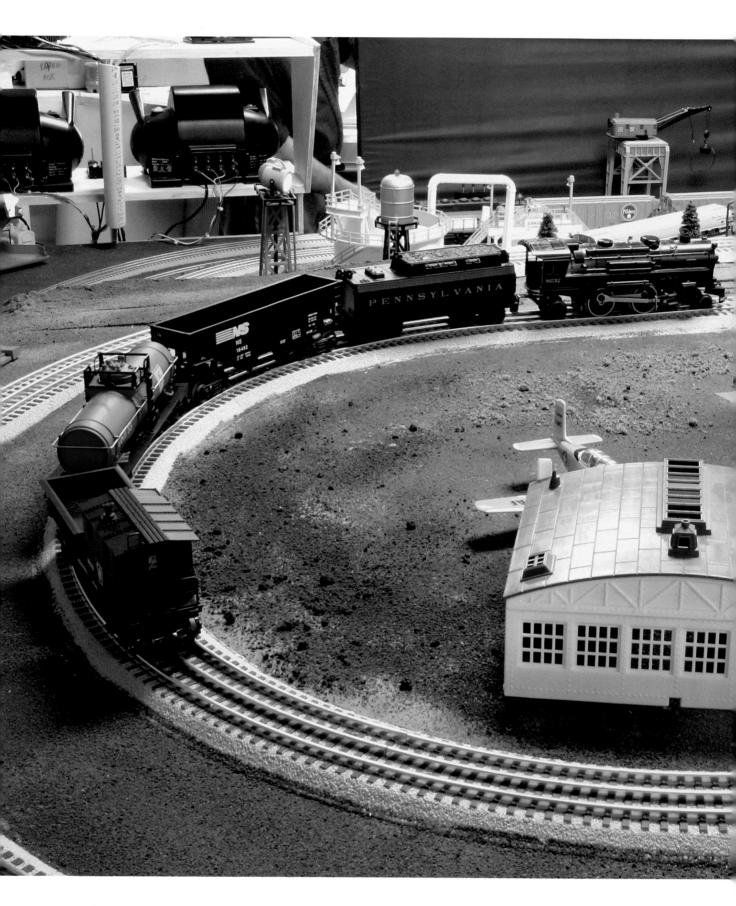

A small airport fills the second loop on the upper level.

Four of the Lionel Action Carnival accessories: 6-24179 Scrambler, 6-24139 Duck Shooting Gallery, 6-34190 Carousel, and 6-24161 Test O' Strength on the upper level.

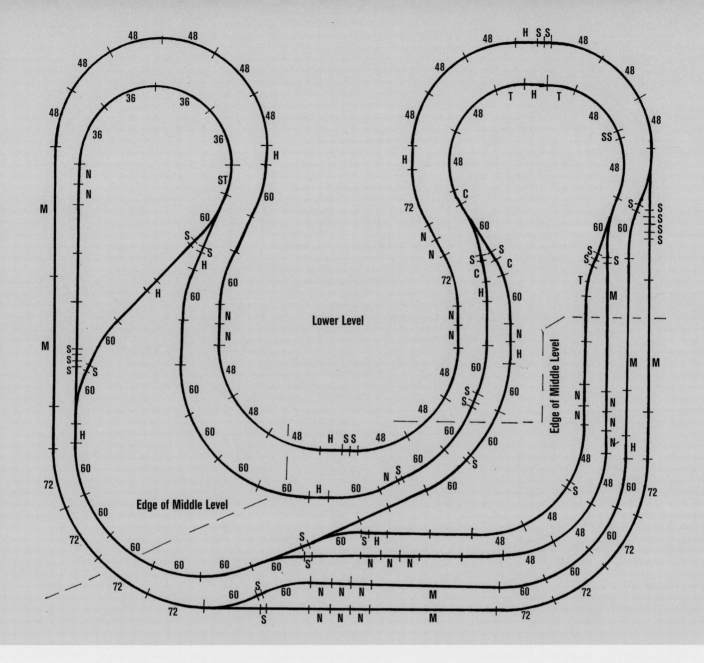

Les Kushner's 12x12 Three-Level Layout – Lower Level

Quantity	Symbol	Part No.	Description
17	None	6-12032	10-inch standard straight
7	M	6-12042	30-inch straight
10	H	6-12024	1/2 straight
20	N	6-12025	4 1/2–inch straight
29	S	6-12073	1 3/8-inch insulated straight
4	36	6-12015	36-inch curve (036)
1	ST	6-12022	1/2 of 36-inch curve (036)

Quantity	Symbol	Part No.	Description
2	C	6-12023	1/4 of 36-inch curve (036)
28	48	6-12043	48-inch curve (048)
20	60	6-12056	60-inch curve (060)
2	60	6-12057	060, a 60-inch switch left
6	60	6-12058	060, a 60-inch switch right
3	T	6-12055	1/2 of 72-inch curve (072)
10	72	6-12041	72-inch curve (16 per circle) (072)

Space required is 12x12 feet.

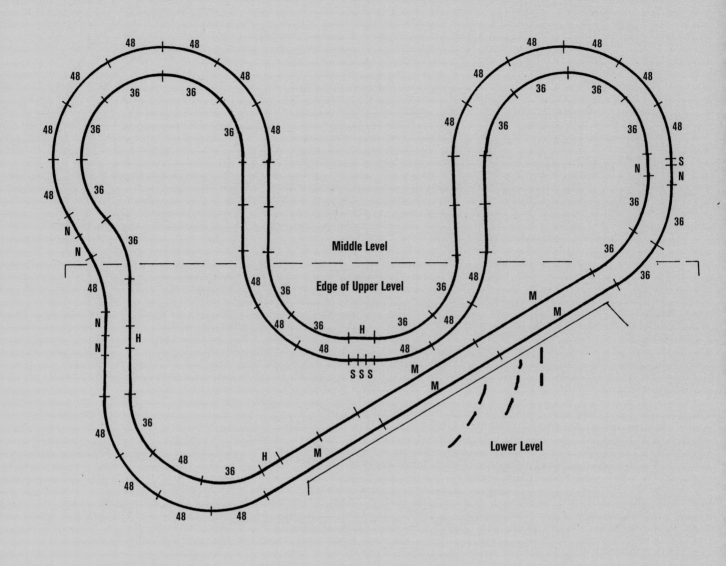

Middle Level

Edge of Upper Level

Lower Level

Les Kushner's 12x12 Three-Level Layout – Middle Level

Quantity	Symbol	Part No.	Description
13	None	6-12032	10-inch "standard" straight
5	M	6-12042	30-inch straight
2	H	6-12024	1/2-straight
6	N	6-12025	4 1/2-inch straight
4	S	6-12073	1 3/8-inch insulated straight
1	ST	6-12022	1/2 of 36-inch curve (O36)
20	36	6-12015	36-inch curve (O36)
25	48	6-12043	48-inch curve (O48)

Space required is 12x9 feet.

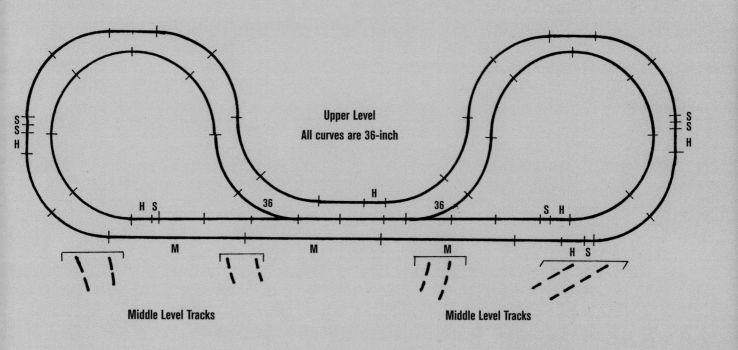

Upper Level

All curves are 36-inch

Middle Level Tracks

Middle Level Tracks

Les Kushner's 12x12 Three-Level Layout – Upper Level

Quantity	Symbol	Part No.	Description
5	None	6-12032	10-inch "standard" straight
3	M	6-12042	30-inch straight
7	H	6-12024	1/2-straight
7	S	6-12073	1 3/8–inch insulated straight
0	ST	6-12022	1/2 of 36-inch curve (O36)
30	36	6-12015	36-inch curve (O36)
1	36	6-12045	36-inch switch left (O36)
1	36	6-12046	36-inch switch right (O36)

Space required is 12x5 feet.

CHAPTER 13

Bill Langsdorf's 14x16 Lionel Legacy Control System Layout

Bill Langsdorf was one of the first to build a large layout using FasTrack, and his model railroad is featured in *The Lionel FasTrack Book*. Since that book was published, he has relocated some of the track and added some simple scenery, as well as the Lionel Legacy Control System to supplement his existing Lionel TrainMaster Command Control (TMCC), as described in Chapter 2.

The layout has two levels with an outer oval and inner reverse-loop-to-reverse-loop track similar to that on the middle level of Les Kushner's layout in Chapter 12. There are crossovers, however, so trains can travel from the inner loop to the outer oval. The lower level has two large outer ovals and a smaller inner oval. When the layout was built, the upper and lower levels were connected, but that incline was one of the tracks that Bill removed. There are several through sidings on the lower level, so opposing trains can pass. There are also about a dozen stub-ended sidings to serve Lionel's animated industries. Bill did not need or want a track plan. Like many Lionel railroaders, he preferred to work in three dimensions using actual track sections on the tabletop.

The tables for the layout are assembled from 1x4-inch boards with 2x4 legs and a ⅝-inch-thick plywood tabletop. The tabletop is covered with a 1-inch-thick layer

Facing page: Four Lionel illuminated station platforms with passengers from Preiser figure sets.

Bill Langsdorf didn't use a plan for his layout, but you can orient most of the photos by using the yellow Lionel Hell Gate Bridge (upper right) as a reference point. Bill relocated the bridge from the front of the layout as it was pictured in *The Lionel FasTrack Book*. This is the revised city on the upper level.

of pink extruded Styrofoam. The layout is divided into eight separate tables, as illustrated in *The Lionel FasTrack Book*, so it can be disassembled for moving.

Bill combined the Legacy System with his existing TMCC, as shown in Chapter 2, and divided the tracks into four electrically isolated blocks, each with unique power needs. Track 1 is powered by a TPC3000 with two 180-watt PowerHouses attached. Track 2 is powered by a TPC400 with two 180-watt PowerHouses attached. Tracks 3 and 4 are powered by Power Masters with 135-watt PowerHouses attached. Each of the four tracks is connected via a power supply with a 6-34120 Direct Lockon for FasTrack. A 275-watt ZW Power Supply powers all the accessories and lights.

Lionel locomotives are massive, and the trains they pull are heavy, so a lot of power is needed. Bill's layout is larger than most Lionel layouts and requires a host of Lionel electrical devices. There are photos of his electrical systems in Chapter 2. Bill is using these items to provide control for four 12-car trains and several dozen lights and accessories:

1	6-14295	990 Legacy Command Set
1	6-14294	993 Legacy Expansion Set
1	6-12911	Command Base
3	6-12868	Remote Controller
2	6-14179	TPC 400
4	6-22983	180-watt PowerHouse
2	6-12867	Power Master
2	6-12866	135-watt PowerHouse
4	6-34120	Direct Lockon for FasTrack

A new industrial area has been created on the 6x8-foot corner. The Hell Gate Bridge is in the upper center.

Scenery construction is underway with a mountain made from cardboard strips glued in a lattice framework with brown painted plaster cloth cover.

The angles of the Lionel 6-12050 22 1/2-degree Crossing match those of the 6-12047 Wye Switch (072), so Bill installed one of the crossings on the far end of the right pair of passenger tracks on the lower level.

Bill used two of Lionel's 6-12047 Wye Switches (072) at the entrance to his four-track passenger station area on the lower level.

He uses a 4250 Power Supply for all of the Lionel Controllers that allow the Legacy System's CAB-2 to control the accessories and switches.

2	6-14181	Action Recorder Controller
1	6-14183	Accessory Motor Controller
1	6-14182	Accessory Switch Controller
3	6-14185	Operating Track Controller
7	SC-2	TMCC SC-2 Switch Controller

The layout is wired with single-strand 18-gauge standardized color-coded wire for track, with red for hot power, black for ground power, white for signal returns, and green for accessories. There are multiple power connections, spaced about every 20 feet of track with connections to most sidings, all connected via a terminal block (barrier strip) wired to the 6-34120 Direct Lockons. He uses 22-gauge four-wire white-jacketed cables (red, green, black, and yellow) to connect the switches and accessories to the power supply. The wires are routed through ⅝-inch holes in the 1x4-inch boards of benchwork or gathered in ½-, 1-, or 2-inch insulated pipe holders. He uses electrical-wire markers on each individual wire for proper identification. The wire markers are also applied near every switch, engine, and accessory so the numbers can be seen to keypunch into the handheld CAB-1 or CAB-2 Remote Controls when he is operating the layout.

Top: The Lionelville Esso Gas Station (6-24183) is busy filling up a Welley-brand toy 1965 Pontiac GTO while a Humble Oil Tractor Trailer (6-12837) pulls out. Notice the Industrial Gas Tanks (6-14143) in the background.

Middle and bottom: The 6-24105 FasTrack Track Gang workers are animated to re-create the work needed to repair a section of track.

CHAPTER 14

Mark Cavaliere's 16x21 Appalachian Empire

Mark Cavaliere dreamed of building this layout since he was in grade school. He saw the plan for an HO layout in a magazine and knew at once that it was the layout he wanted. Several decades passed, and Mark became a Lionel fan with a large collection of locomotives and cars, but his only layout was assembled at Christmas from the Lionel Steel Tubular Track on the floor of his den. He didn't have enough time to build anything more complex.

Buying Your Dream Layout

Mark discovered that there were custom-layout builders who could build his dream layout. He talked with Doug Waller at the Train Station in Mountain Lakes, New Jersey, who translated his HO dream layout into this 16x21-foot empire that just fit his available space. Steve Sherman and his Custom Train Layouts crew then translated the plan into wood, Styrofoam, and FasTrack reality. In truth, the layout was still in the assembly stage when the photographs were taken—the crew had another week or so of detailing and wiring to complete it. The layout was actually built and finished inside the Custom Train Layouts shop then disassembled into sections and transported to Mark's home. There was no mess in his house, and he had absolute proof that if he ever needed to move the layout, it could be disassembled and reassembled.

Because the Custom Train Layouts crew has perfected its techniques, they can work more efficiently than an amateur.

Facing page: The scenery is carved blue Styrofoam, as described in Chapter 5.

The 6x8-foot corner of Mark Cavaliere's layout is devoted to Lionel action industries like the Log Loader and Icing Station.

Most of these techniques are shown and described in Chapters 3, 4, 5, and 6.

The track plan is extremely complex. Trace around it with a pencil or your fingertip, and you will see that this is, essentially, a single-track oval that is very convoluted. There is a reverse loop on the lower level inside the main line, but it is an optional route. There are also cutoff tracks that allow the tracks in the upper right of the upper level to be operated as a reverse loop. There is also a five-track yard and a three-track industrial area. Since the layout is being operated with the Lionel Legacy Control System, trains can follow each other around the layout. There are also two through sidings (parallel or concentric pairs of tracks with switches at both ends), so the trains can pass one another when traveling in opposite directions.

Real Railroad Operations

This layout is unusual for a Lionel model railroad, because it does not include two or four or six completely independent routes for the trains. This layout is similar, however, to thousands of HO scale layouts where their builders wanted to emulate the single-track main lines of many real railroads. Since the source for this plan was an HO scale layout, the single-track main line is no surprise. Layouts of this style try to include as many running feet of track as possible in the available space. The operations around the figure eight–style portion of the layout in the upper right of the plan are an example: Trains traveling clockwise around the outer track on the far-left side of the layout enter the figure eight complex and run diagonally from upper

The majority of the layout is visible looking across the five-track yard, with the mountain section in the upper right.

left to lower right on the inside track; then loop counterclockwise 270 degrees back over the entry track from the upper right to lower left to swing around 270 degrees clockwise to the outermost track at the top of the plan; then around the outer track 180 degrees to head out of the figure eight complex. That's about three laps of the same space. The two pairs of switches that connect the inner and outer curves at the far upper right allow those tracks to do triple duty as run-through tracks as just described, as a passing siding for the inner track, and to allow a reverse loop for trains running counterclockwise.

The five stub-ended sidings in the lower left and the four tracks that feed into them also emulate HO model railroad practice. A FasTrack 6-12020 Uncoupling Track is installed at the beginning of each of the stub-ended sidings, so the sidings can be used to rearrange the cars from inbound freight trains, just as similar tracks are used on real railroads. There is one long pair of tracks with switches at each end in the center of the layout that allows a freight train arriving counterclockwise (right to left) to stop, so the locomotive can uncouple from the train. The locomotive can then run forward through the left switch then reverse to back along the adjacent parallel track to run around the train. The locomotive can then pull forward through the switch behind the train to couple onto the rear of train, allowing the locomotive to push the train into any of the five stub-ended sidings in the lower left. These through sidings that allow the trains access to stub-ended sidings are called run-arounds. The

train can be pushed whole or one car at a time, with each car being placed on a different siding.

The three parallel tracks in the lower left of the plan serve a different purpose. These are designed and spaced to feed Lionel action accessories like the Log Loader and Coal Elevator. Again, industrial yards are a common design element on HO scale layouts. The plan provides the opportunity to re-create the operations of complete through-freight and passenger trains moving both "eastbound" and "westbound," as well as freight yard and industrial yard operations. The spectacular scenery makes those operations even more credible.

This valley is spanned with a series of two Lionel Girder Bridges, a Lionel Truss Bridge, and a second Lionel Girder Bridge.

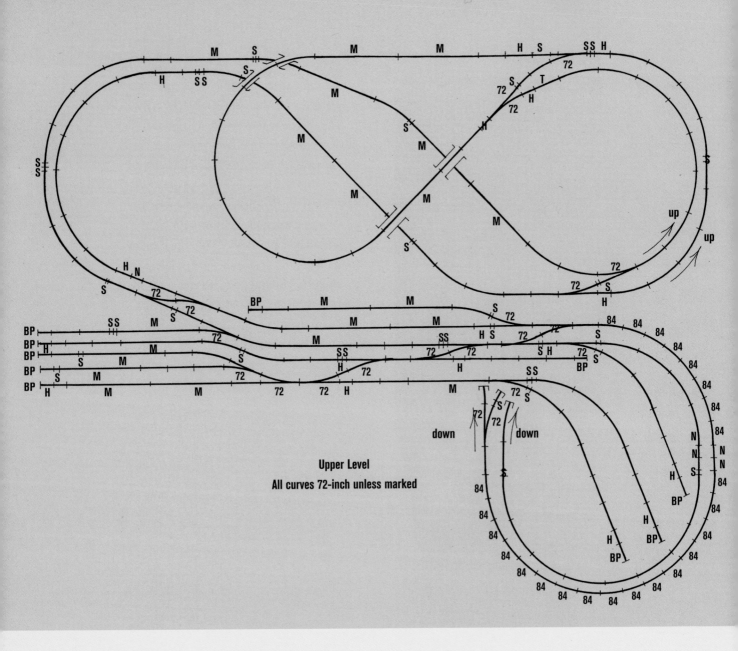

Upper Level

All curves 72-inch unless marked

Mark Cavaliere's 16x21 Appalachian Empire

Quantity	Symbol	Part No.	Description
46	None	6-12032	10-inch "standard" straight
24	M	6-12042	30-inch straight
15	H	6-12024	1/2-straight (5-inch)
5	N	6-12025	4 1/2-inch straight
38	S	6-12073	1 3/8–inch insulated straight

Quantity	Symbol	Part No.	Description
9	BP	6-12035	Lighted Bumper or
	BP	6-12059	Earthen Bumper
98*	None	6-12041	72-inch curve (072)
13	72	6-12048	72-inch switch left (072)
7	72	6-12049	72-inch switch right (072)
24	84	6-12061	84-inch curve (084)

Space required is 16x21 feet.

*Note: All curves are 72-inch, except for the 270 degrees of 84-inch curve in the lower right, and the tracks to two hidden reverse loops join at "A" and "B" on the plan.

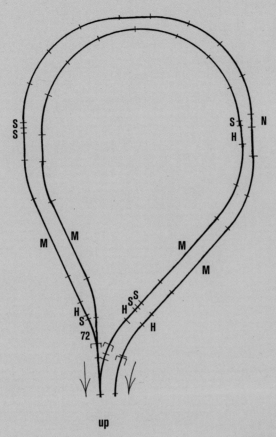

up

Lower Level
(All hidden beneath upper level)
All curves are 72-inch

Looking across the industrial area to the mountains in the upper right of the plan, the stacks of extruded blue Styrofoam that shape the mountains are visible—that opening is a removable access hatch that will be covered with a ski lift area.

The backside of the layout (upper edge of the plan) is covered with 2-inch-thick sheets of blue Styrofoam placed vertically. The rocks were carved with a hot knife; the surface was coated with spackling plaster and was painted and dry-brushed by the Custom Train Layouts crew. The holes in the far left are for access to the two loops of track on the lower level.

The mountains are a series of sheer cliffs on the back side of the layout (the upper edge on the plan). This is Lionel's massive replica of the EMD SD90MAC Diesel.

The parallel tracks leading into the five-track yard are a realistic scene. The layout was still in the process of being wired, so the blue tags identify wiring locations to connect the controls.

A Lionel Lighthouse and Ocean Shore occupy the lower-left corner of the 6x8-foot industrial corner of the layout.

The curves and switches are all 72 inches or larger, so the longest Lionel locomotives, like the SD90MAC diesel, and cars can operate without derailing.

CHAPTER 15

Doug Waller's 9x12 Mountain Layout

Doug Waller, like many Lionel fans, had been putting off building his Lionel layout for years. With FasTrack, however, he realized that the work of adding ties and ballast, as required with the older all-steel track, was no longer necessary. He had a 9x12-foot room available, so he created a simple two-level track plan. There are only two switches, all the curves are 36 inches, and most of straight tracks are 30-inch 6-12042 FasTrack sections.

The tables are two 4x8-foot pieces of ½-inch plywood with a 2x2-foot piece separating them to form a U shape. The 4x8 table on the right is 5½ inches lower than the table on the left, because all of the lower-level tracks are on the right side of the layout. The only upper-level track on the right side of the layout is supported by the simulated steel piers in Lionel's 6-12755 Elevated Trestle Set. A 1x4 wood ramp carries one lower-level track upgrade across the 2x2 section and up to the left half of the layout. He cut off a 2-foot corner of the right table to install a handmade wood trestle (see Chapter 4).

The upper level is simply an oval bent into a U shape. A single track descends from the center on one side of the oval to a reverse loop on the lower level. The reverse loop will only reverse trains traveling in a clockwise direction around the upper level. Trains traveling counterclockwise must be backed though a lower-level reverse loop to change direction. The layout is operated with Lionel TrainMaster Command Control, so there is plenty of room for running two trains at once.

Facing page: Doug Waller's 9x12 layout is built on two levels with a 4x8 table on the left 5 1/2 inches higher than the 4x8 table on the right. A ramp leads across the 2x2 table in the center to carry the lower-level track to the upper level.

The scenery construction has just begun. The mountain in the corner of the layout is a stack of 11 layers of 2-inch Styrofoam carved and shaped with a hot knife.

The scenery shapes are covered with a layer of plaster mixed with paper mache pulp, then painted with a brown stain.

The vertical faces of the upper level will be covered with Scenic Express flexible stone walls.

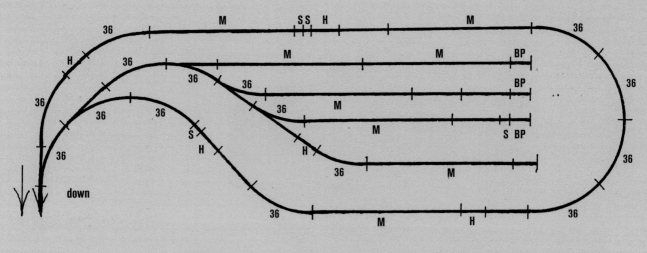

Upper Level